BRADFORD TRANSPORT

DAVID J. CROFT

AMBERLEY

First published 2010

Amberley Publishing
Cirencester Road, Chalford,
Stroud, Gloucestershire GL6 8PE

www.amberleybooks.com

Copyright © David J. Croft 2010

The right of David J. Croft to be identified as the
Author of this work has been asserted in accordance
with the Copyrights, Designs and Patents Act 1988.

ISBN 978-1-4456-0158-8

British Library Cataloguing in Publication Data.
A catalogue record for this book is available from the
British Library.

Typeset in 10pt on 12pt Sabon.
Typesetting and Origination by FONTHILLDESIGN.
Printed in the UK.

Contents

Introduction and Acknowledgements

Bradford, like many provincial towns and cities, has changed dramatically over the last 150 years. The skyline of this Yorkshire city, once the centre of the world's wool textile industry, has changed forever with the loss of its mill chimneys. Gone too are many of the grand Victorian buildings such as Kirkgate Market, Swan Arcade and the Mechanics Institute. People from around the world have made it their home, and in so doing have altered the appearance of the city's streets. And of course the transport has changed. The passage of time has seen the arrival and departure of stage coaches, horse buses, horse trams, steam trams, electric trams, charabancs and trolleybuses. We are left with the all-conquering motor bus. However, this does not mean that these forms of transport are forgotten. Bradfordians are very proud of their city's past and its transport heritage, and it is hoped that this book will bring back memories of days gone by and also introduce younger generations to a city and its transport, when going out for a trip by charabanc or catching the 'trackless' were a way of life.

This is not intended to be a detailed account of the history of Bradford's public transport. Other books have already done this, and a number are listed at the end of this book.

In selecting the illustrations, I have tried to cover the main aspects of the city's transport and I have also tried to include some of the more unusual subjects, hence the chapter on miscellaneous vehicles.

The majority of the illustrations are from my own collection, built up over a period of forty years or so, and it has not proved possible to identify the photographers in some cases. To those whose work is not individually credited, I offer my apologies.

A number of people must receive special thanks for making this book possible: Susan Caton, from the Local Studies Department of Bradford Central Library for allowing me to search through the library's photographic collection and to select a number of images for inclusion in the book which are reproduced by permission of Bradford Libraries, Archives and Information Service. Don Akrigg and Roy Marshall for allowing me to include photographs from their extensive collections. John Hansen for digitising the bulk of the illustration, and Sarah Powell, who helped with those from the library's collection. And finally, thanks go to Campbell McCutcheon and the team at Amberley Publishing for putting the book together.

Compiling it has been a real journey of nostalgia, and even I learned a few things along the way! Any errors in the text are solely my responsibility, and I apologise in advance.

David Croft
Bradford
July 2010

CHAPTER ONE

Horse-Drawn Transport

Although stage coaches had provided long-distance transport in the Bradford area from 1789 to 1844, there were no organised local services until 1864. There were of course horse-drawn cabs and carriages available for hire, but these would have been beyond the means of most of the population. It is reported that the Bradford Livery Stable Company introduced the city's first horse bus service in December 1864, and over the next few years the number of services increased. By 1872, horse bus services were being provided to Allerton, Four Lane Ends, Idle, Lister Park, Bankfoot and Thornbury. These ran chiefly from the New Inn at the end of Thornton Road, or from the new Exchange on Market Street. This network had expanded still further by 1888 with additional services to Bolton Woods, Denholme, Wilsden, Dudley Hill, West Bowling, Queensbury and Eccleshill. Although these services were no doubt appreciated by the public, they were operated by individual concerns and the frequencies were irregular. Most used converted waggonettes with bench seating. Those to West Bowling, however, were double-deck buses with transverse 'garden seats' on the top deck and were identical to those used in the capital by the London General Omnibus Company.

The introduction of horse trams along Manningham Lane in 1882 brought about the first organised public transport service to Bradford, but due to the hilly nature of the city, horse trams were not suitable for other routes. Nevertheless, the horse trams were popular and ran until the end of January 1902, when they were replaced by Corporation electric trams.

The city's last horse buses ran to West Bowling in 1904.

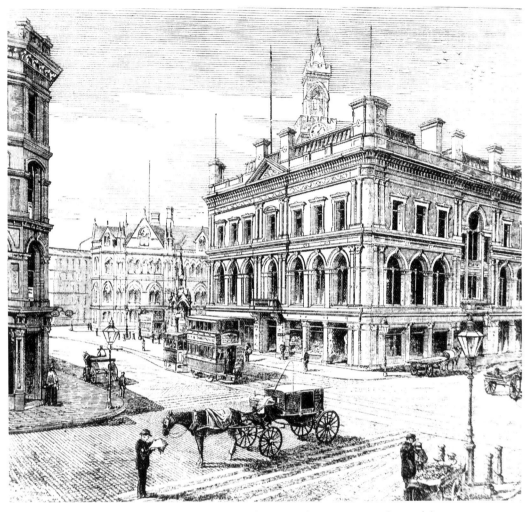

Bridge Street in around 1888 with a horse-drawn cab waiting for customers and one of the new-fangled steam trams outside the Mechanics Institute. (*Bradford Libraries*)

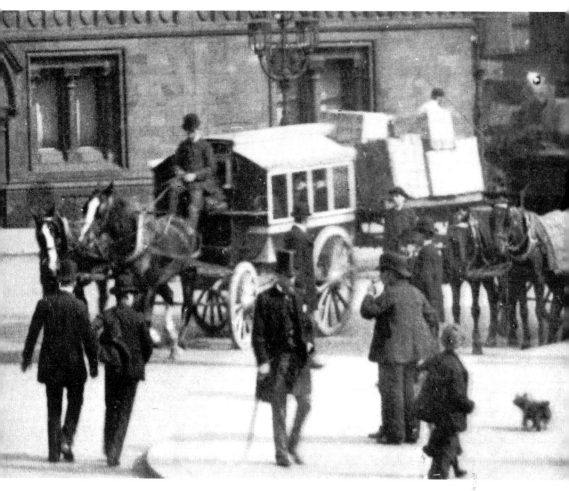

A horse bus sets out from Town Hall Street in around 1891. In 1972, the street was renamed Channing Way and was pedestrianised in 2010. (*Bradford Libraries*)

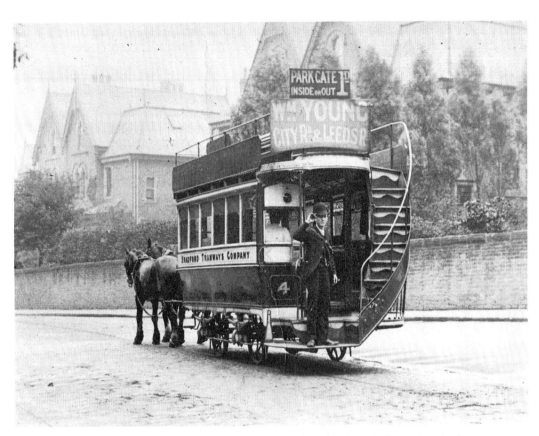

Horse tram no. 4 of the Bradford Tramways Company stands at the Lister Park terminus in the 1880s. The fare was originally 2*d*, but it was later reduced to 1*d*. How often does that happen nowadays? (*Bradford Libraries*)

CHAPTER TWO

Steam in the Streets

Steam trams were seen as a more suitable form of transport for hilly places such as Bradford. These provided a smoother ride at greater speed plus the ability to carry more passengers. The first steam trams were introduced in the city in 1882 by the Bradford Tramways & Omnibus Company, the operator of the Manningham Lane horse trams. Routes were opened along Leeds Road and Thornton Road in 1882, to Undercliffe and Frizinghall in 1888, and to Dudley Hill in 1893. A separate company, the Bradford & Shelf Tramway Company, began operating steam trams up Manchester Road as far as Bankfoot in 1884. These were subsequently extended to Shelf in 1886 and to Wyke in 1893.

Although the steam trams provided regular and reliable services to many parts of Bradford, they were prone to accidents and during their twenty-year existence there were numerous mishaps and runaways, some spectacular and some unfortunately fatal.

With the introduction of Corporation-owned electric trams from 1898, the steam trams were largely replaced in 1902, though they were retained on the Bankfoot–Shelf section until 1903.

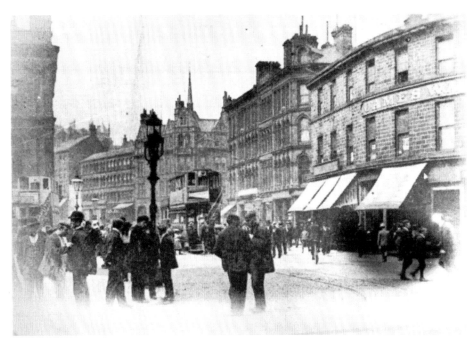

A busy scene in Bridge Street in the 1890s with a steam tram on the service from Leeds Road to Four Lane Ends. (*Bradford Libraries*)

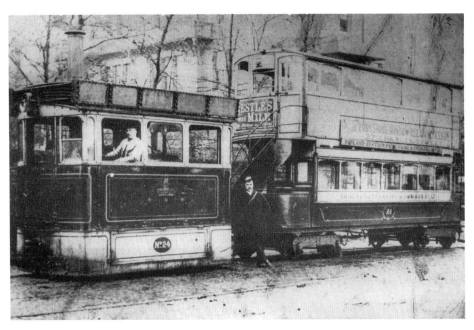

Waiting to depart from Frizinghall is steam tram locomotive no. 24 and trailer car no. 28 of the Bradford Tramways & Omnibus Company on the route across the city to Undercliffe in around 1889. (*Author's collection*)

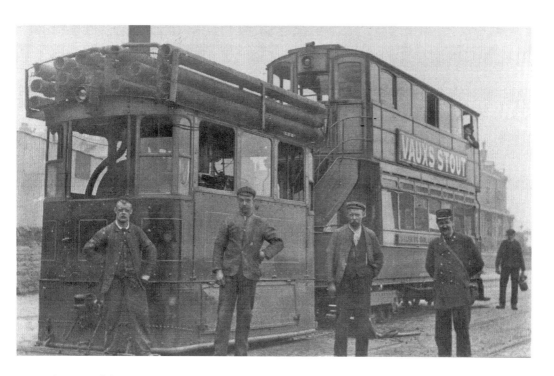

The crew of this steam tram pose for the photographer at Saltaire before they begin the journey back to Undercliffe. This service operated between 1888 and 1902. (*Author's collection*)

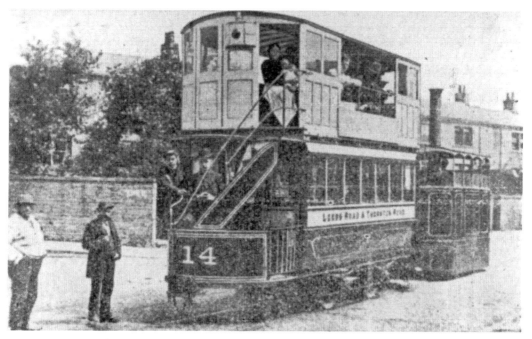

Four Lane Ends terminus in around 1884. Note the mother and baby on the top deck – an unusual sight in Victorian times. Perhaps it's the driver's wife. (*Author's collection*)

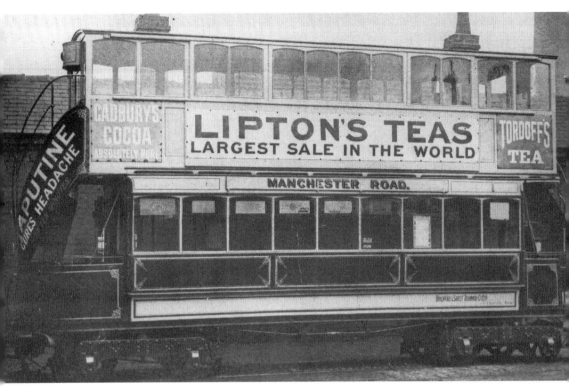

A close-up view of one of the Bradford & Shelf Tramways Company steam tram trailers outside Bankfoot depot. The Manchester Road steam tram services were replaced by Corporation electric trams in 1902-03. (*Author's collection*)

CHAPTER THREE

Electric Trams

Transport technology was advancing rapidly in the 1880s and 1890s and before long the horse and steam trams were seen as old-fashioned compared with the newly developing electric trams.

An experiment with an electric tram took place in 1892 in Bradford's Cheapside. Michael Holroyd Smith of Halifax had built the electric tramway on Blackpool Promenade in 1885 and he was keen to demonstrate this new form of transport. Although the experiment seems to have been a success, it was not until 1898 that electric trams were introduced in Bradford.

Bolton Road and Great Horton Road were the first to benefit from the Corporation's new electric trams. Gradually the system was extended to serve Lidget Green, Duckworth Lane, Stanningley and Thornton (1900), Manningham Lane and Wakefield Road (1902), and Bowling Old Lane and Bradford Moor (1904).

For a period of less than a year, the neighbouring town of Shipley had its own electric tramway system. This was operated by the Mid-Yorkshire Tramways Company with routes from Thackley to Nab Wood and from Baildon Bridge to the Branch Hotel. The company was not a financial success, and it was taken over by Bradford Corporation in April 1904 and the routes were integrated into the city system.

In 1906, Leeds City Tramways suggested that a through service of electric trams should be operated between the two cities. However, Leeds used the standard gauge 4 ft 8½ in gauge, whereas Bradford used the narrower 4 ft gauge. C. J. Spencer, the Bradford tramways manager, set about designing a special axle that could be fitted to trams, enabling the change of gauge to be negotiated at Stanningley. This proved to be a success, and from 1909 to 1918 a jointly operated through service was provided and was the only example of its kind ever to be used in Britain.

Between 1910 and 1931, the Corporation built over a hundred new tramcar bodies at its Thornbury Workshops, and although all appeared similar, there were differences in height, width and length. An experimental single-deck tram was also constructed in 1927, but this had a short life, and was withdrawn in 1931.

During the 1930s and 1940s, most tram routes were converted to either motor bus or trolleybus operation, and the city's last trams ran on 6 May 1950. The very last tram, no. 104, is preserved at the Bradford Industrial Museum at Moorside Mills, Eccleshill.

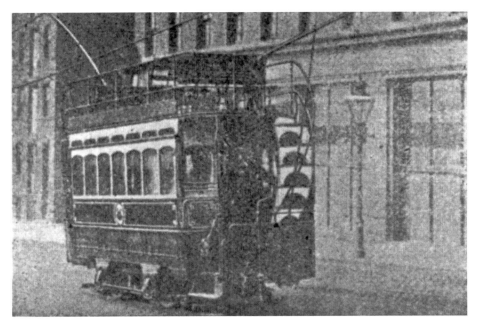

An experimental electric tram was demonstrated for several months in 1892 on a route between Forster Square and North Parade. Although the trials were deemed to be a success, it was not until 1898 that electric trams made a return to Bradford. The tram is seen here ascending Cheapside. (*Author's collection*)

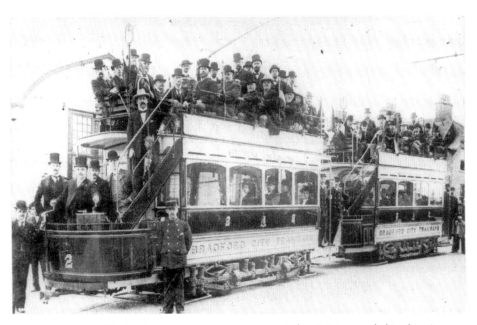

The opening of Bradford's electric tramway system on 29 July 1898 is recorded in this view taken outside Bolton Depot. (*Author's collection*)

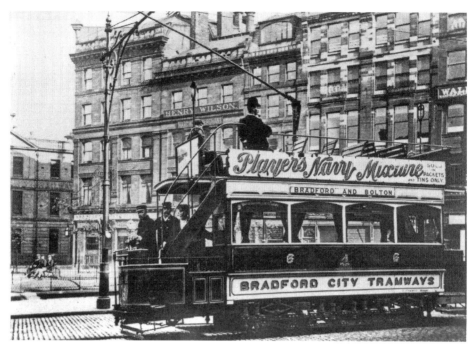

Forster Square, 1901. Tram no. 6 was built in 1898 and is about to depart to Bolton Junction. (*Author's collection*)

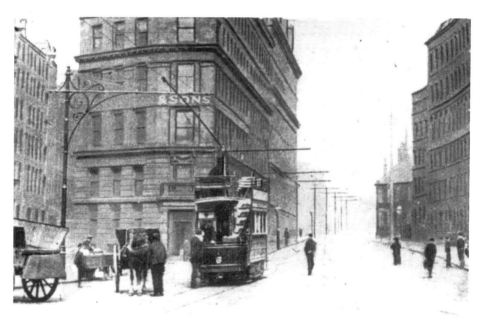

Another view of car no. 6 at the bottom of Bolton Road. The building behind the tram became the Transport Department's head office in 1929. (*Author's collection*)

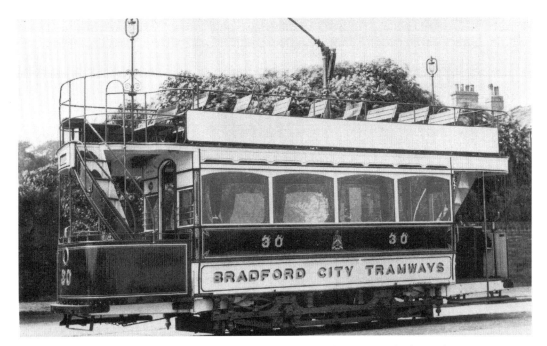

In 1900, Bradford purchased a batch of twenty-five open-top trams from the Brush Electrical Engineering Company of Loughborough and these were numbered 29-53. No. 30 is seen here when new. What would today's health and safety people make of that open balcony? (*Roy Marshall, Omnibus Society*)

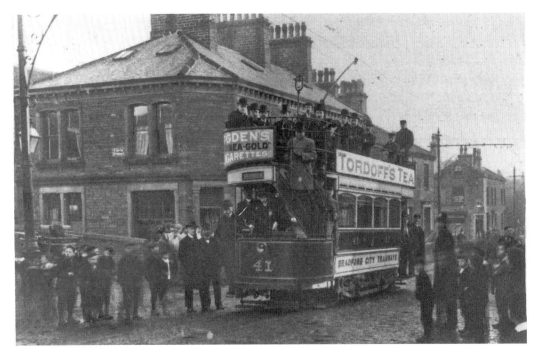

The opening of the tram route to Thornton on 18 December 1900 attracts much attention from the local children. Tram no. 41 was in service until April 1929. (*Author's collection*)

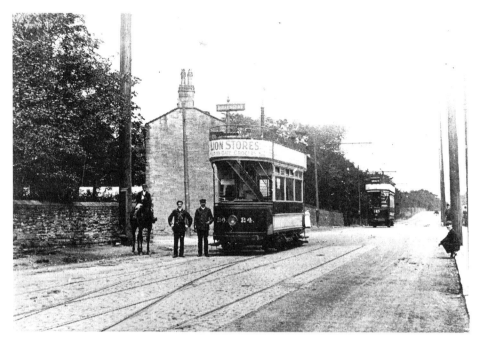

Birkenshaw tram terminus, 1903. In the foreground is Yorkshire Woollen tram no. 24 with Bradford's no. 163 in the background. Through running between the two systems was prevented by different track gauges. (*Bradford Libraries*)

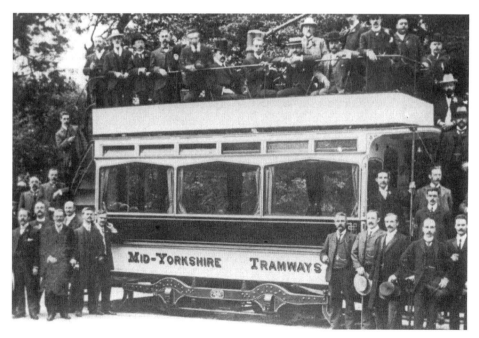

The opening of the Mid-Yorkshire Tramways at Nab Wood on 23 July 1903. This small system, which had ten trams, was purchased by the Bradford Corporation on 30 April 1904. (*Author's collection*)

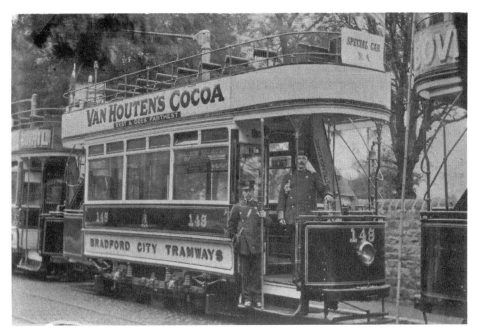

The Bradford Exhibition, held in Lister Park during the summer of 1904, attracted thousands of visitors and necessitated extra tram services. Here, tram no. 148 of 1902 stands in North Park Road with its smartly dressed driver and conductor. (*Author's collection*)

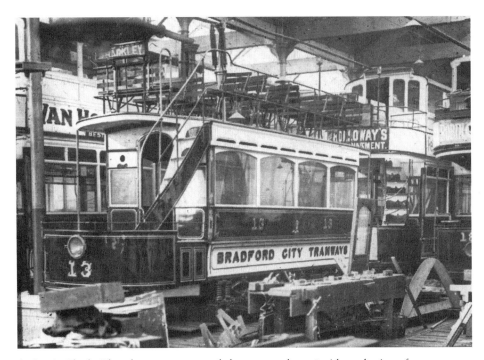

A view inside the Thornbury tramway workshops around 1906 with a selection of trams including no. 13 receiving attention. (*Author's collection*)

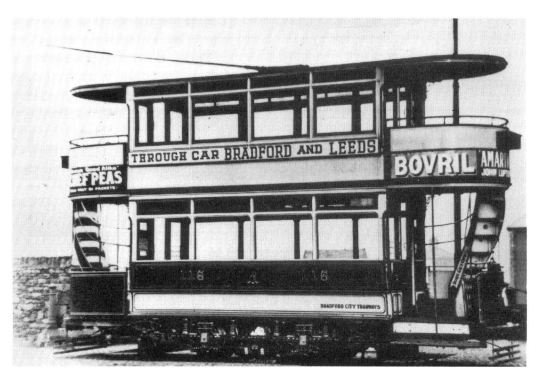

Tram no. 116 of 1902 was one of ten Bradford trams fitted with dual-gauge trucks to allow through running to Leeds. The service ran spasmodically until 1918. (*Author's collection*)

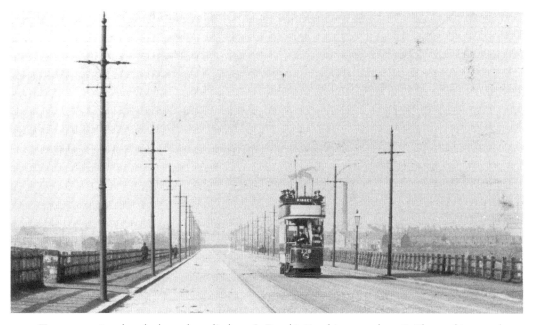

Tram no. 138 makes the long slow climb up St Enoch's Road in around 1908. The road is named after alderman Enoch Priestley, who fought for the provision of a tram service to Wibsey. (*Author's collection*)

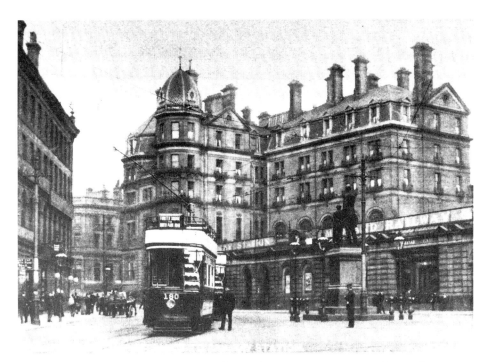

A tranquil view of Forster Square in around 1910 showing tram no. 180 waiting to depart to North Park Road, a short-working on the Heaton route. The Midland Hotel and the entrance to what was then Market Street Station form the background. (*Bradford Libraries*)

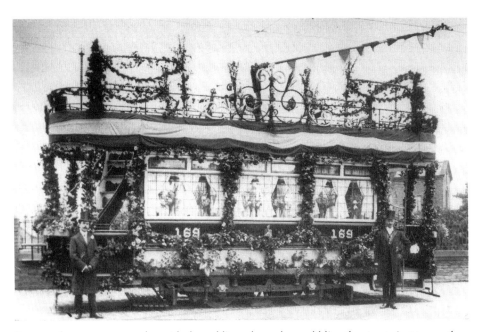

Decorated trams were popular with the public and people would line the streets just to see the trams pass by. Here is no. 169 decorated for the Tramways Department sports day in 1911. (*Author's collection*)

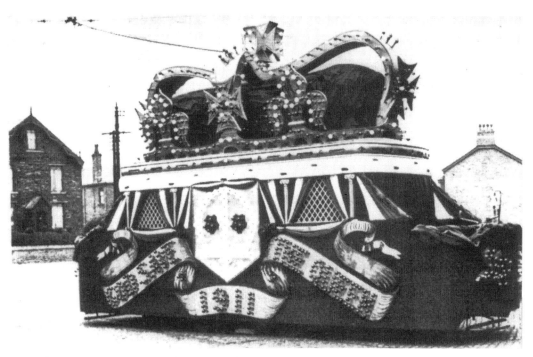

The June 1911 coronation of King George V and Queen Mary was celebrated by the construction of this illuminated tram, which was used for other events in later years. (*R. B. Parr Collection*)

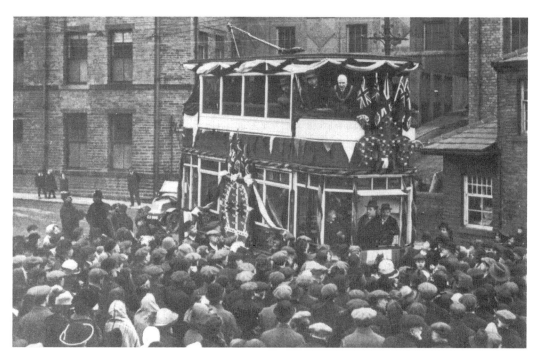

Tram no. 229 of 1912 decorated for the extension of the route from Wyke to Bailiff Bridge on 17 May 1913. Note the variety of hats! (*Author's collection*)

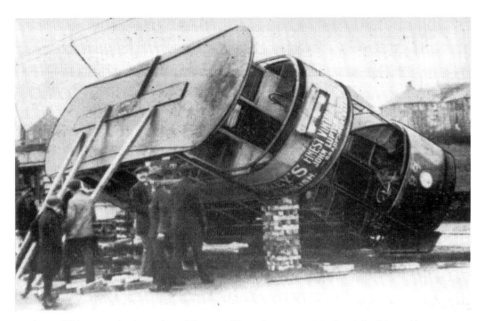

No heavy lifting gear in those days! The re-railing of tram no. 88 after it had been blown over by the wind at Allerton on 8 February 1913. (*Author's collection*)

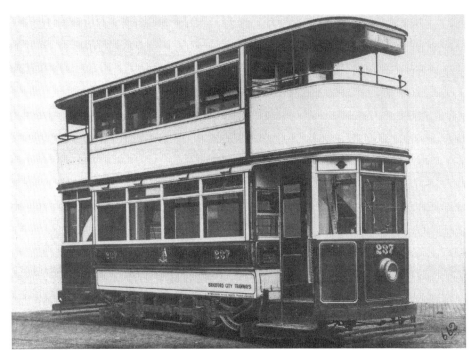

Between 1919 and 1921, the Corporation took delivery of forty-six trams built by English Electric of Preston. Seen here when new, no. 237 ran in Bradford until 1942, when it was one of a number sold to Sheffield to help replace trams destroyed in the bombing of that city. (*Roy Marshall, Omnibus Society*)

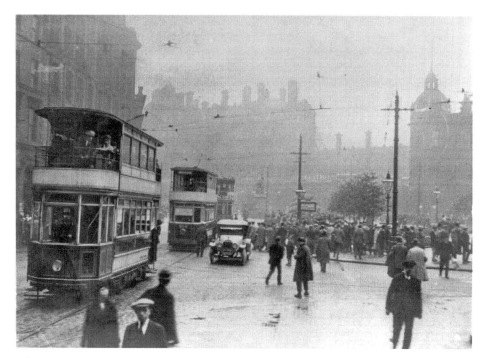

A busy scene in Forster Square in around 1920. New passenger queue barriers were installed in 1922 to separate them from the traffic. The tram at the back is still in wartime grey livery. (*Author's collection*)

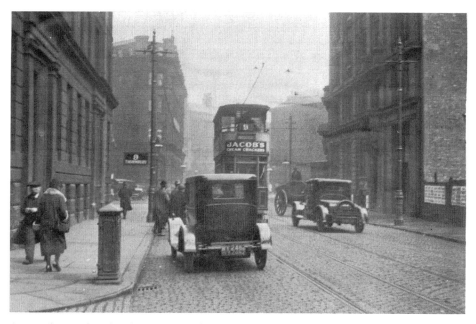

A tram departs for Thornbury in around 1920 amid the warehouses and offices of Leeds Road. The interesting motor car on the right seems to be getting a bit close to the horse and cart. (*Author's collection*)

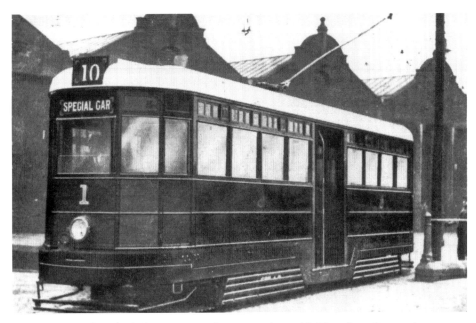

The experimental single-deck tram no. 1 of 1927 stands outside Thornbury Depot when new. It only ran in service until 1931, when it was sold for use as a bungalow at Reighton Gap, near Filey, where it remained for a further fifty years. (*Author's collection*)

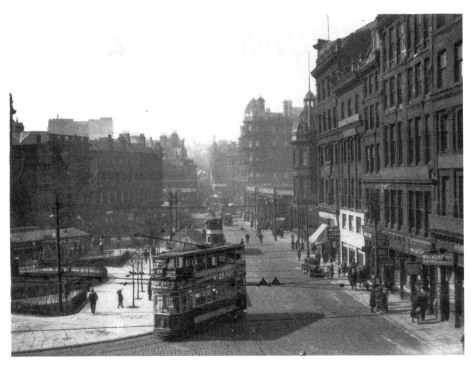

Forster Square, 1931. Tram no. 11 sets out on its journey to Bingley. The buildings on the right were destroyed by fire in June 1950. (*Author's collection*)

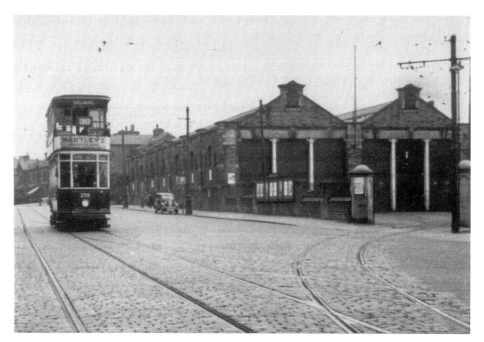

Saltaire tram depot in 1938 with tram no. 239 about to make the journey across the city to Bradford Moor. (*Author's collection*)

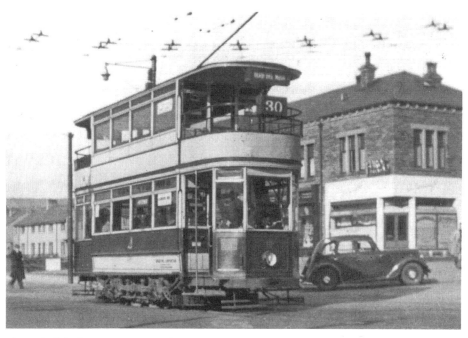

The end of the line in more ways than one. This is Crossflatts terminus on 1 May 1939, just days before the trams were replaced by trolleybuses. The tram, no. 111, was built in 1926 and ran for a further ten years until 1949. Beyond here was West Yorkshire bus territory. (*Author's collection*)

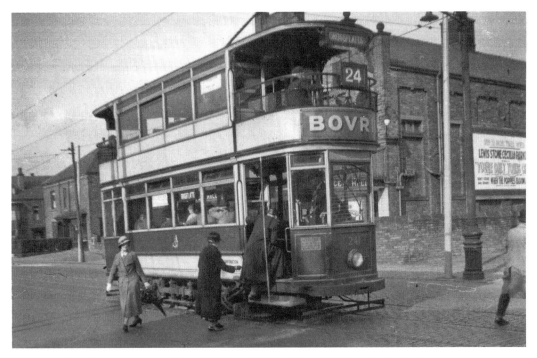

Passengers board tram no. 241 at Prince's Hall on Bradford Road, Shipley, during its journey to Crossflatts on 6 May 1939, the last day of tramway operation on the Manningham Lane routes. Trolleybuses took over the following day. (*Author's collection*)

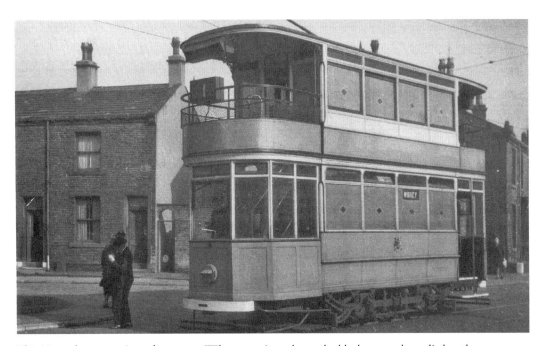

This November 1941 view of a tram at Wibsey terminus shows the blackout mesh applied to the windows, the masked headlight, and white-painted step edges and bumper. (*E. Thornton*)

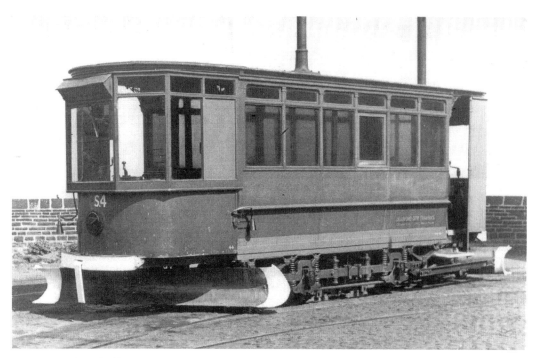

A number of older trams were converted for use as works trams. Here is snowplough tram S.4 outside Horton Bank Top depot in September 1943. It began life as tram no. 133 in 1902. (*E. Thornton*)

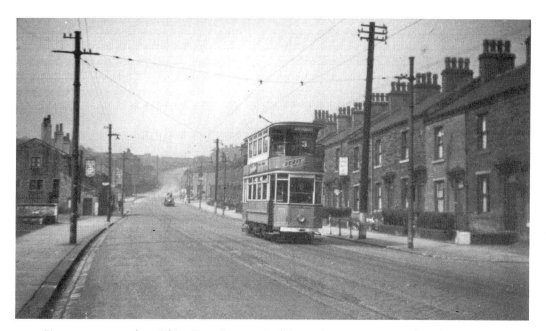

Tram no. 109 stands at White Horse in 1945. It claims to be going to Queensbury but it's facing the wrong way. The author lives just up the hill in the background and wishes Great Horton Road was as peaceful as this today! (*Author's collection*)

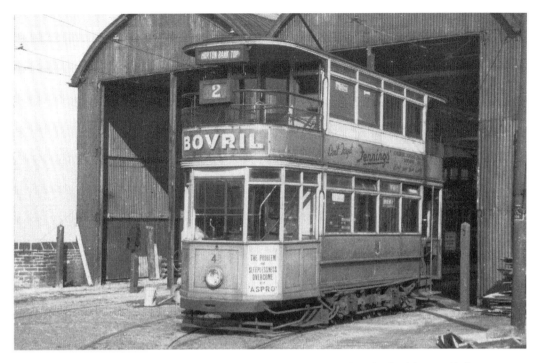

Tram no. 48 rests outside Horton Bank Top depot in 1948. It is painted in the final livery of lighter blue and cream. (*R. F. Mack*)

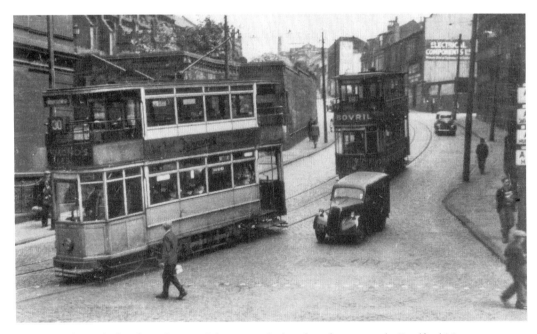

Two trams descend Church Bank on 23 July 1949 – the last day of trams on the Bradford Moor route. A temporary service of motor buses took over the following day until trolleybuses began in December. Note the soot-blackened cathedral on the left. (*Author's collection*)

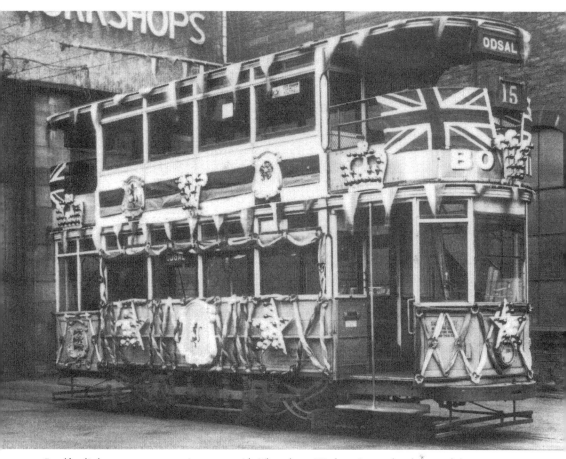

Bradford's last tram, no. 104, is seen outside Thornbury Works prior to the closure of the tramway system on 6 May 1950. (*Bradford Libraries*)

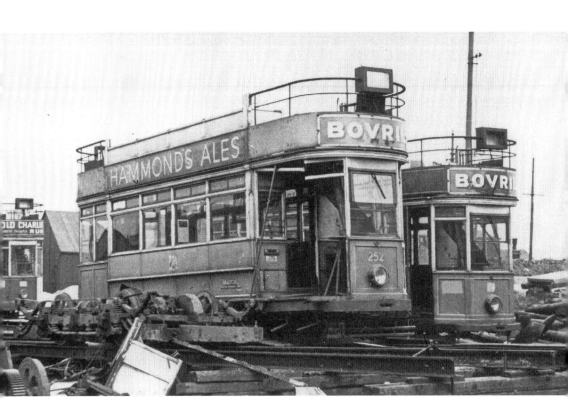

Following the closure of the tramway system, these trams are in the process of being broken up in the permanent way yard at Bowling depot later in the year. (*R. F. Mack*)

CHAPTER FOUR

Trolleybuses

Bradford and Leeds were the first places in Britain to operate trolleybuses, both systems being opened simultaneously on 20 June 1911. Bradford's first route ran from Laisterdyke to Dudley Hill, and expansion of the system continued throughout the 1920s. The Corporation built the first two top-covered, double-deck trolleybuses to be used in Britain, and also introduced a number of one-man-operated, single-deck trolleybuses, which were used on the less busy routes until 1931.

During the 1930s, the trolleybus network expanded as more tram routes were replaced, including the routes to Saltaire via Thackley (1930), Thornton (1934), Duckworth Lane (1935), and Crossflatts and Tong Cemetery (1938).

The post-war years saw a further period of development, with new routes and vehicles. Several former tram routes were converted to trolleybus operation, notably to Bradford Moor (1949), Thornbury (1952) and Wibsey (1955), and other routes were extended, the last being to Buttershaw (1956) and Holme Wood (1960).

The 1950s and 1960s were notable for the acquisition of many second-hand trolleybuses. Between 1953 and 1961 no fewer than eighty-five such vehicles appeared on the city's streets, notably from Notts & Derby, Llanelly, Darlington, St Helens, Brighton, Hastings, Doncaster and Mexborough. Many ran in original condition but some were fitted with new, modern front-entrance bodywork as were many older native Bradford vehicles.

While many other transport undertakings gave up using trolleybuses and turned to motor buses, Bradford seemed able to keep them viable, but redevelopment of the city centre plus cheaper oil prices were used as reasons for abandoning this efficient, pollution-free form of transport. The decision to abandon the trolleybuses came in 1962 and the Bradford Moor and Eccleshill to St Enoch's Road Top services closed that same year. These were followed by the Manningham Lane services in 1963, the Bolton-to-Bankfoot service in 1964, and the Wakefield Road services in 1967. After a gap of four years, the conversion programme began again in 1971 with the conversion of the routes to Allerton, Clayton, Saltaire via Thackley, Greengates, Wibsey and Buttershaw. This left only the cross-city Thornton to Thornbury and the busy Duckworth Lane routes to be operated by trolleybuses, and normal service on these routes ended on Friday 24 March 1972.

Two days of special trolleybus tours then followed. Transport enthusiasts from around the country flooded into the city to witness the end of Bradford's, and Britain's last, trolleybus system. Following a final gathering at Thornbury Depot, plus the inevitable speeches, the power was turned off at 5.07 p.m., thus ending sixty-one years of trolleybus operation.

In the years since 1972, various proposals have been put forward for the re-introduction of trolleybuses in Bradford, but ironically it now seems likely that neighbouring Leeds, which began trolleybus operation on the same day as Bradford back in 1911 but abandoned them in 1928, could well be the first to re-introduce them to Britain.

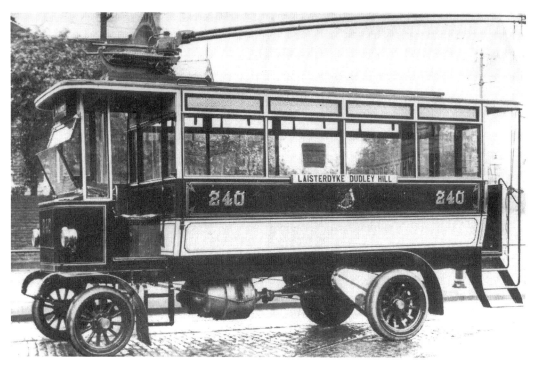

The vehicle that started it all – Bradford's and Britain's first trolleybus, no. 240 – stands at the Dudley Hill terminus of the route to Laisterdyke in 1911. (*Author's collection*)

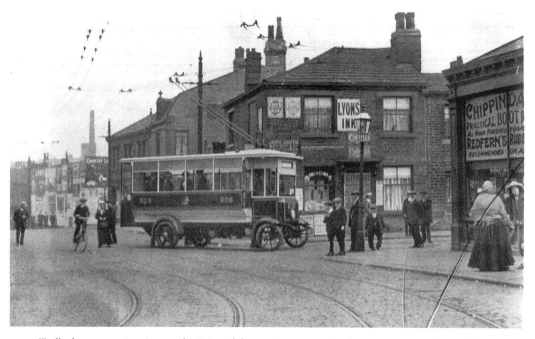

Trolleybus no. 506 arrives at the Laisterdyke terminus sometime between 1911 and 1914. The photographer appears to be attracting more attention than the trolleybus. (*Author's collection*)

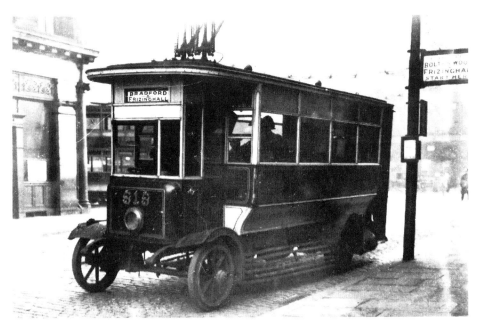

Trolleybus no. 515 of 1914 stands in Canal Road in around 1923 with Forster Square in the background. The route to Frizinghall had opened in 1915 and was replaced by West Yorkshire buses in April 1932. (*Bradford Libraries*)

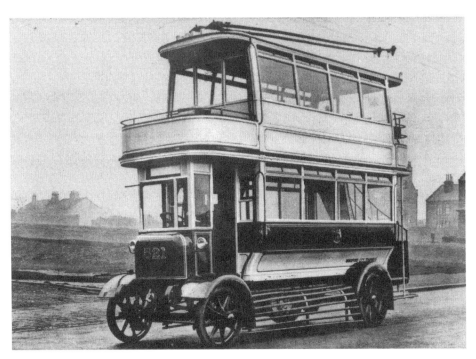

Bradford Corporation's 521 was the world's first top-covered double-deck trolleybus. It was built at Thornbury Works in 1920 and ran in service until 1928. It is seen here in Killinghall Road when new. (*Bradford Libraries*)

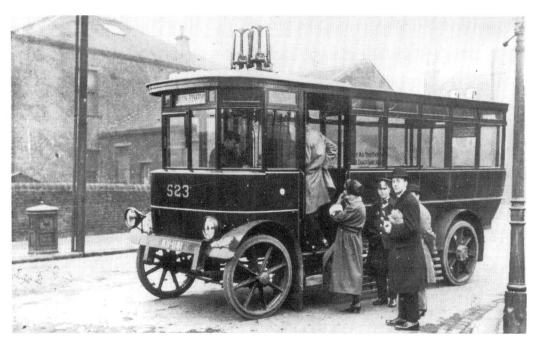

Paying the driver is not new. This was one of six trolleybuses built at Thornbury Works in 1922/23 for use on the Bolton–Bankfoot route. It is seen here at Laisterdyke in its original varnished teak livery. It ran until 1930. (*Author's collection*)

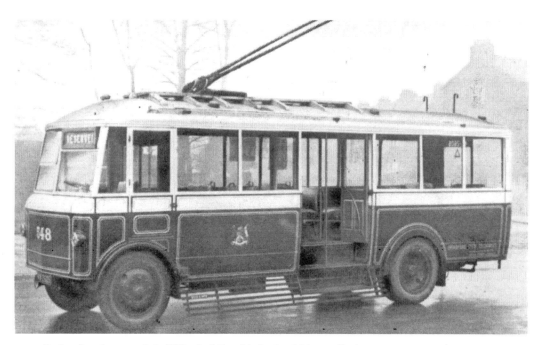

Posing for photograph in Killinghall Road is Leyland Lion trolleybus no. 548, one of seventeen delivered in 1928-29 with centre-entrance bodywork by English Electric. It ran in Bradford for just ten years. (*Author's collection*)

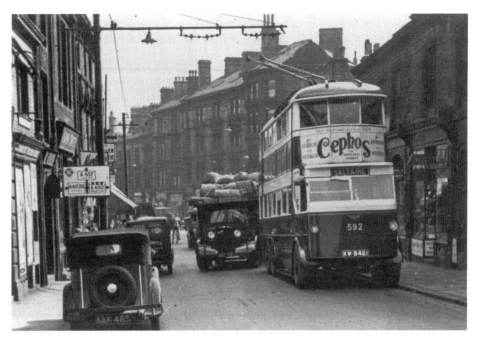

The driver of this wool lorry is anxious to overtake trolleybus no. 592 in Briggate, Shipley, probably in the late 1930s. The bus was new in 1931 and is on the long route from town to Saltaire via Bolton Junction, Thackley and Windhill. Fox Corner is in the background. (*Author's collection*)

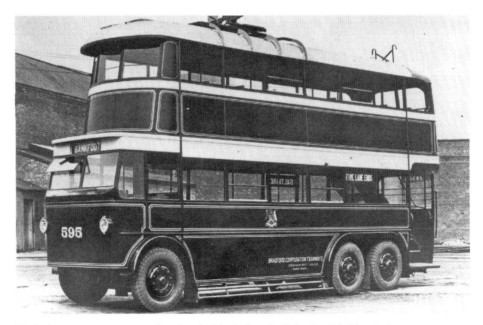

Trolleybus no. 595 was one of twelve double deckers built by English Electric in 1930-31. These vehicles were said to be very hard to steer and were not popular with the drivers. It was withdrawn from service in June 1942. (*Author's collection*)

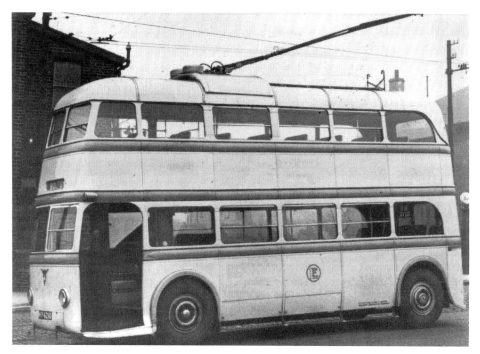

Meet 'Queenie' – the very latest in trolleybus design in 1934. Only five of these AEC Q-type trolleybuses were built and only two ran in Britain. This one became Bradford's no. 633 and ran until 1942, when it was sold to the South Shields Corporation. (*Author's collection*)

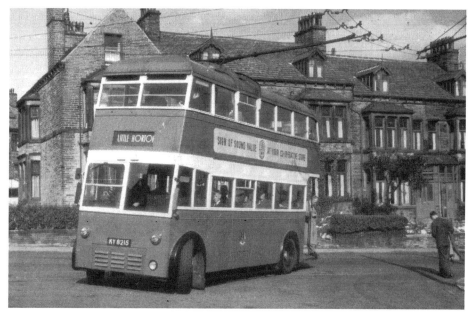

New in 1934, trolleybus no. 612 was re-bodied in 1944 with this utility body by Brush. It is seen here on an enthusiasts' tour on 16 September 1956 turning from Toller Lane into Little Lane – despite showing 'Little Horton' on the destination blind. (*Author's collection*)

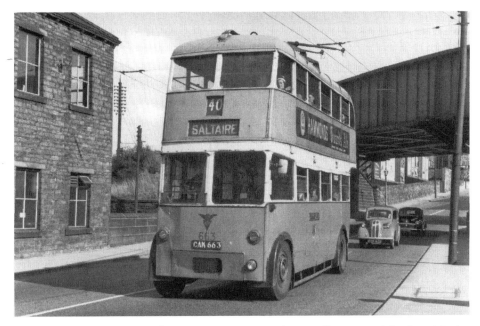

AEC trolleybus no. 663 entered service in May 1939 and ran until 1957, retaining its original English Electric body to the end. It has just negotiated the low railway bridge at Windhill on its way to Saltaire on the long route 40 from town via Thackley and Shipley. (*R. F. Mack*)

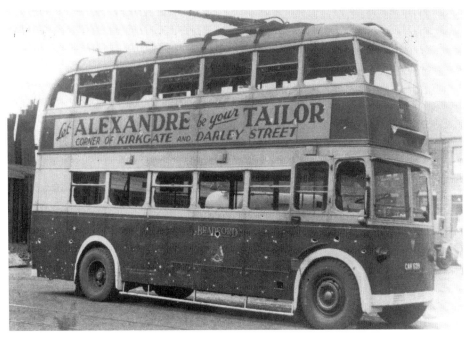

Safely back at Thornbury Works, trolleybus no. 639 was one of three damaged by shrapnel during an air raid on 31 August 1940 while parked in the city centre. It was soon repaired and returned to service. (*Author's collection*)

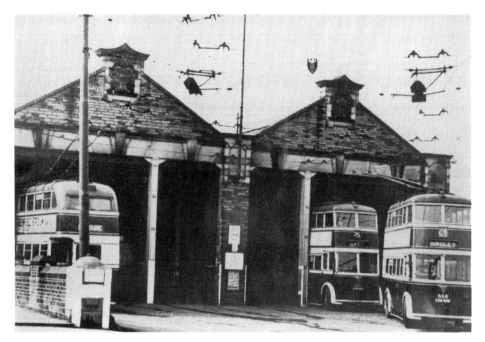

Saltaire depot in use by trolleybuses during the Second World War. Note the white-painted mudguards and the shields above the overhead points to prevent flashes being seen by enemy aircraft. (*Author's collection*)

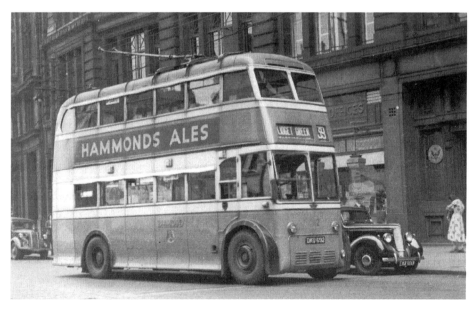

Trolleybus no. 692 is on its way from Thornbury depot to take up service on the Lidget Green route. It was originally a Karrier demonstrator and entered service in Bradford in 1940. A new Crossley body was fitted in 1952. The lady on the right appears to have lost something in her handbag – perhaps it's her gas bill, as she is almost outside the Corporation's Gas Department in Britannia House. (*Author's collection*)

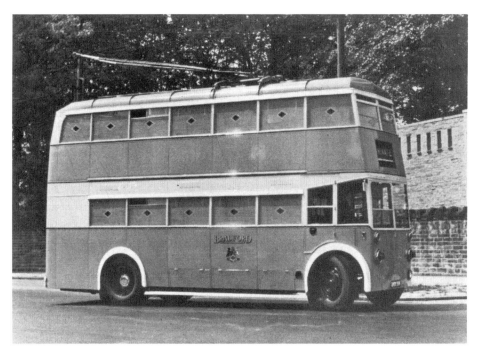

Seen at Nab Wood when new in 1942 is trolleybus no. 694, one of ten Sunbeam MF2s intended for export to Johannesburg but diverted to Bradford due to the war. The utility bodywork is by Weymann, and like all other buses in wartime it had white-painted mudguards and anti-blast netting on the windows. (*Author's collection*)

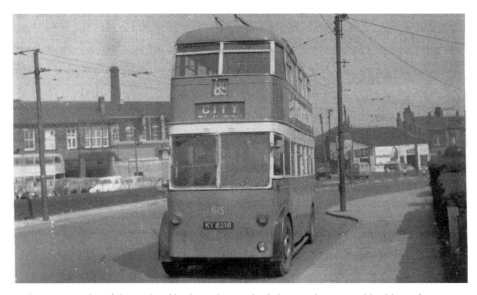

Only six examples of this style of bodywork were built by Northern Coachbuilders of Newcastle, and Bradford took delivery of all of them in 1946 as replacements for pre-war bodywork. No. 615 is seen at Thornbury terminus in the 1950s with the former English Electric factory to the left. (*Author's collection*)

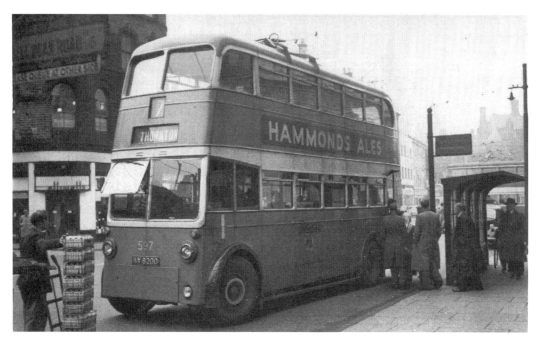

Northern Coachbuilders went on to produce a more stylish body design in 1947-49, and Bradford purchased twenty-one, again as replacements for earlier bodies. No. 597 is seen at the city terminus of the Thornton route in the 1950s. (*Author's collection*)

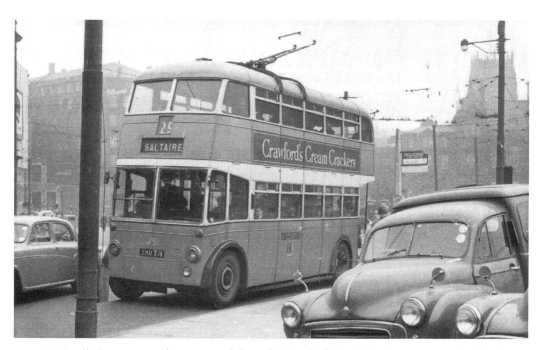

BUT trolleybus no. 751 of 1949, one of the twelve Roe-bodied vehicles that were associated with the Bradford Moor–Crossflatts route for many years, stands in Forster Square on 10 October 1959. (*Author's collection*)

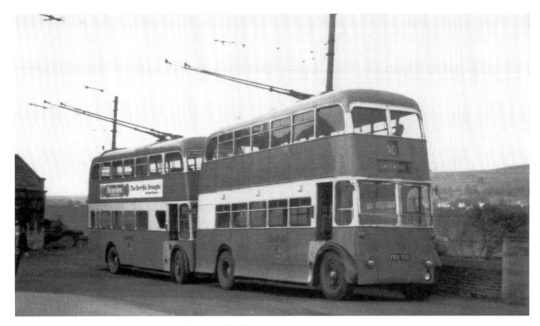

The last new trolleybuses purchased by Bradford were eight attractive Weymann-bodied BUTs in 1951. No. 758 is seen here in the depot yard at Saltaire at the end of a trip from town on route 40 by way of Thackley. (*Author's collection*)

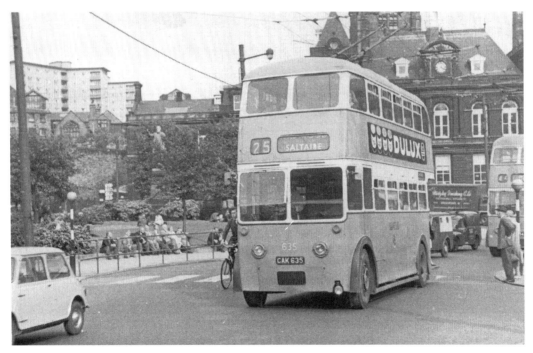

In 1952, thirteen trolleybuses were re-bodied with very distinctive bodywork by Crossley of Stockport. Seen here passing through Forster Square on its way to Saltaire is no. 635. Do you remember when Forster Square was a pleasant place to sit in? (*Author's collection*)

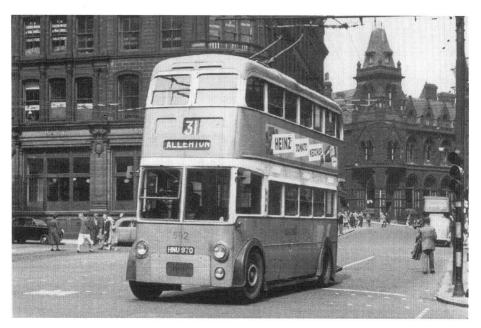

Bradford became famous for its second-hand trolleybuses in the 1950s and 1960s. Here, no. 592, one of thirty-two purchased from the Notts & Derby Traction Company in 1953, turns at the bottom of Sunbridge Road to return to Allerton. It was later fitted with a new East Lancashire body in 1958 and ran until 1968. (*R. F. Mack*)

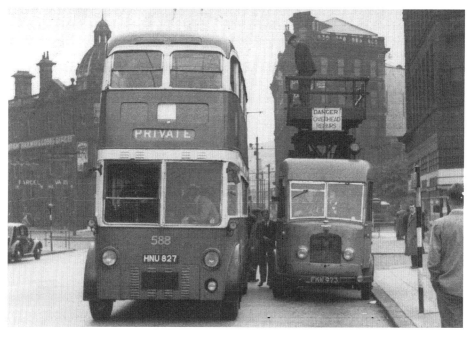

An enthusiasts' tour on 20 June 1954 used former Notts & Derby trolleybus no. 588 to formally open the new wiring along Broadway, which connected Forster Square (in the background) with the rest of the city centre. (*R. F. Mack*)

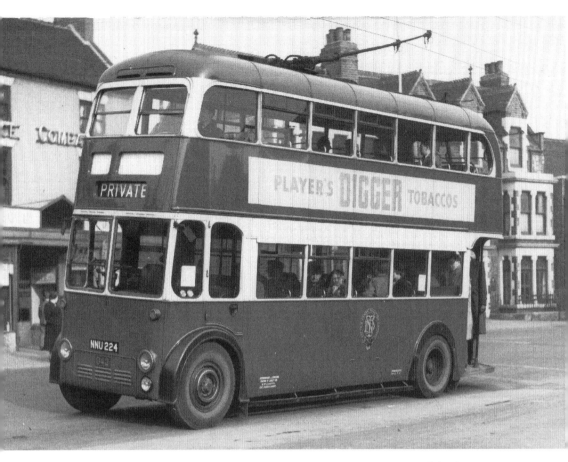

Almost a Bradford bus, but not yet. This Weymann-bodied BUT 9611T was one of the thirty-two vehicles purchased from Notts & Derby in 1953. It is seen here on 15 March 1953 in Market Street, Heanor, on an enthusiasts' tour. It became Bradford no. 760 and ran until 1964. (*R. F. Mack*)

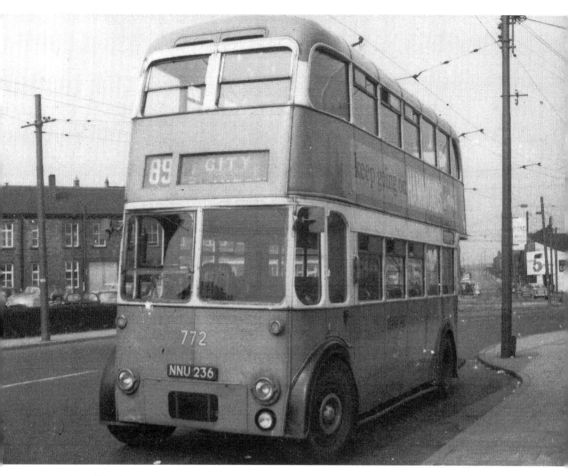

Another of the former Notts & Derby trolleybuses was no. 772, seen here at Thornbury terminus. It had received a revised front destination box layout following a collision early in its life in Bradford. (*D. Akrigg*)

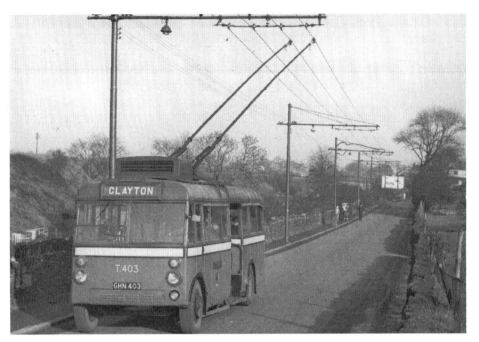

Bradford acquired twenty-four single-deck trolleybuses from the Darlington Corporation between 1954 and 1957. Only this one was running in service in Bradford during the Suez Crisis in 1957, and along with eight others it was fitted with new front-entrance double-deck bodies in 1958/59. It is seen here in Pasture Lane on the Clayton route during an enthusiasts' tour in 1957. (R. F. Mack)

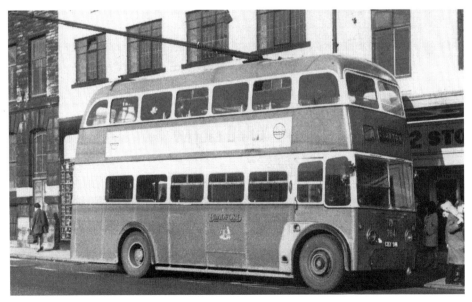

Between 1956 and 1963, Bradford had ninety-eight trolleybuses fitted with new bodywork by East Lancashire Coachbuilders of Blackburn. Here, former Llanelly trolleybus no. 784 stands in Thornton Road having arrived in town from Clayton. (D. Akrigg)

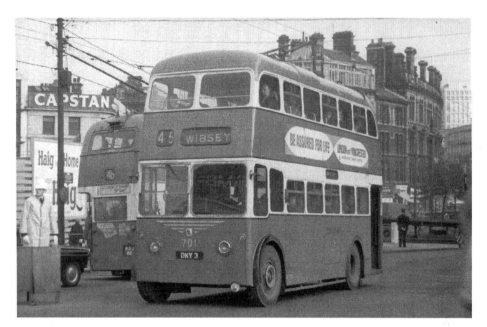

The policeman in his box looks somewhat anxious as he is passed by trolleybuses in Town Hall Square. No. 701, seen here, was one of ten originally destined for Johannesburg in 1942 but delivered to Bradford due to the war. It was re-bodied by East Lancashire Coachbuilders in 1956. (*Author's collection*)

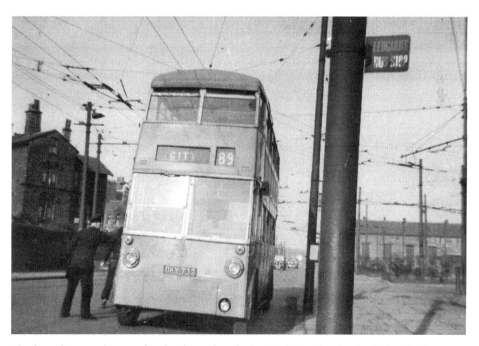

The first photograph ever taken by the author depicts Park Royal utility bodied trolleybus no. 732 outside Thornbury depot. The bus stop sign reminds us that Ledgards ran this way on their service between Bradford and Leeds via Pudsey. (*Author's collection*)

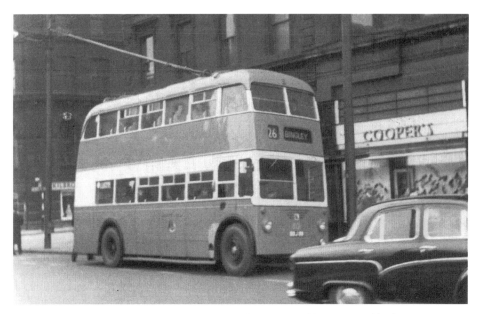

Eight former St Helens trolleybuses were acquired in 1958 and became Bradford nos 794-801. Here, no. 801 stands at the Bingley loading barrier in Forster Square not long before the buildings in the background were demolished to make way for an enlarged square without the trolleys. (*Author's collection*)

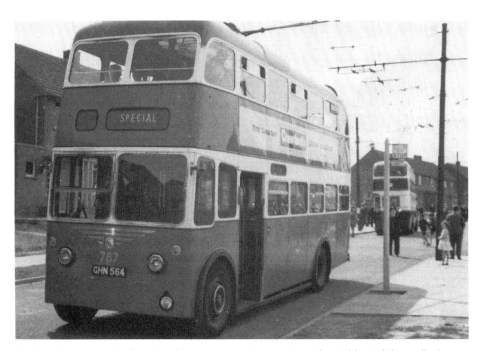

The locals are out in Holme Wood on 20 June 1961 to witness the Golden Jubilee trolleybus cavalcade visit their estate. Dark-blue-liveried no. 687 in the background has just negotiated the reverser while no. 787, a former Darlington single decker re-bodied by East Lancashire, is about to make the same manoeuvre guided by an inspector. (*D. Akrigg*)

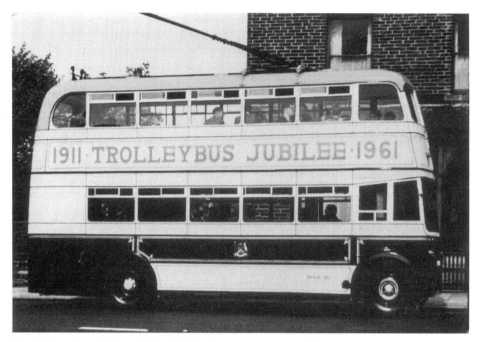

To celebrate the Golden Jubilee of trolleybus operation in Bradford, two trolleybuses were painted in commemorative liveries. Seen here is no. 603 in a representation of the original 1911 livery. This vehicle ran over a million miles in service in Bradford. (*Author's collection*)

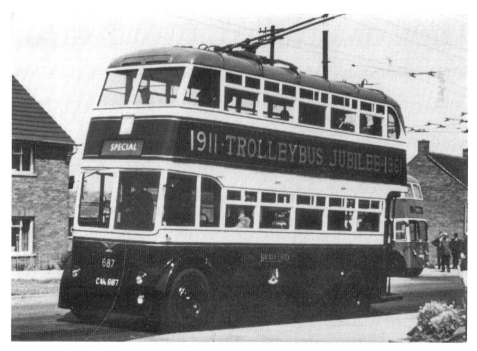

Holme Wood is the location for this photograph of the other trolleybus in Golden Jubilee livery. No. 687 is painted in the 1938 ultramarine blue and cream livery. (*Author's collection*)

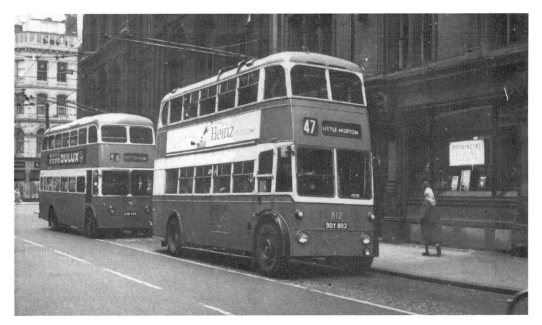

A quiet scene in Tyrrel Street on 6 October 1962 with the Mechanics Institute as background to two second-hand trolleybuses. Former Hastings no. 812 is bound for Little Horton while behind, no. 787, a re-bodied, former Darlington single decker, is going to Buttershaw. (*Author's collection*)

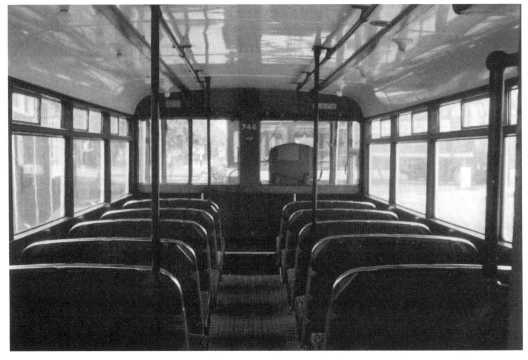

Trolleybus interiors (1). The lower saloon of Roe-bodied BUT trolleybus no. 746 of 1949. (*Author's collection*)

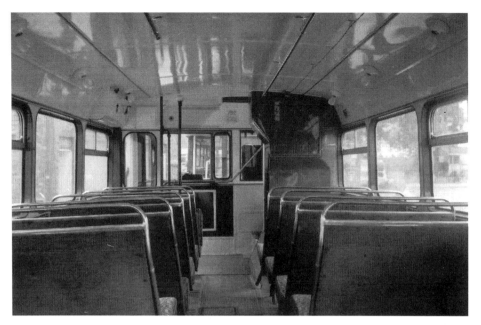

Trolleybus interiors (2). Looking towards the cab of East Lancashire-bodied front-entrance trolleybus no. 792. The bodywork on this vehicle was built in 1959. Notice how much lighter the interior looks, and that metal and plastic have replaced the wood finish of no. 746, seen above. (*Author's collection*)

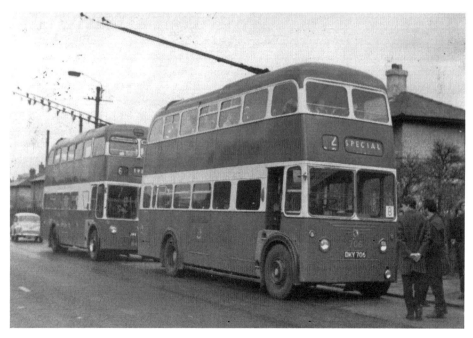

During the final weekend of trolleybus operation, a number of tours were run for the hundreds of visiting enthusiasts. Here, nos 706 and 845 pause at Thornbury terminus for the benefit of photographers. (*Author's collection*)

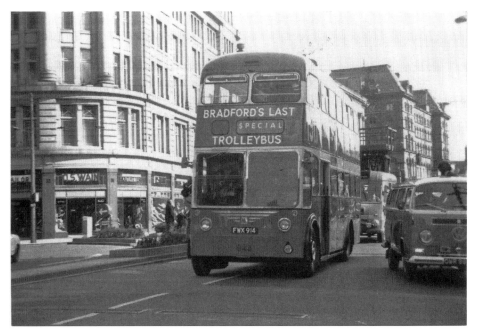

Almost the end. Trolleybus no. 844 heads along Bridge Street to City Hall to commence its final journey on Sunday 26 March 1972. It is being followed by a tower wagon, in case any problems with the overhead wiring are encountered. (*Author's collection*)

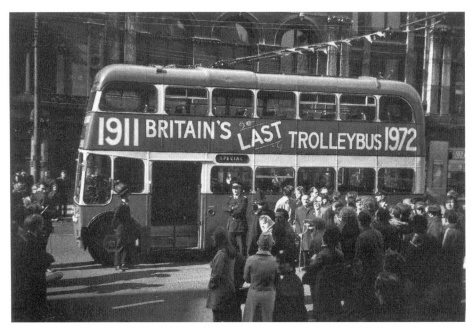

A few minutes later, and no. 844 stands outside City Hall awaiting the civic party for its 3 p.m. departure on the final journey before the trolleybus system closes. (*Author's collection*)

CHAPTER FIVE

Charabanc Days

Fifty years or more before space exploration allowed man to boldly go where no man had gone before, the coming of the charabanc did much the same thing for the working people of our industrial towns and cities. While the trams had enabled people to walk beyond the terminus into the neighbouring countryside, the motor charabanc could take them much further afield to places previously unheard of.

The earliest charabancs arrived on the scene in the years before 1910 and a number of local firms were set up in Bradford including Blythe & Berwick of Charles Street, Hirst Brothers of Dudley Hill, and the Kwick Transport Company of Beckside Road, Lidget Green.

Charabanc trips were popular for Sunday School trips, works outings and sightseeing excursions. Popular destinations from Bradford included Skipton, Grassington, Ilkley, the Goit Stock Waterfalls at Harden, near Bingley, and Sunny Vale Gardens at Hipperholme, near Halifax.

Despite motor vehicle technology being in its infancy, the lack of protection from the weather, and a number of fatal accidents in the Yorkshire area, people were not deterred from taking to the roads. During the First World War, many vehicles were requisitioned for military use and their drivers enlisted. When peace returned in 1918, there was an insatiable demand for coach excursions, and more and more vehicles flooded the market.

However, passengers had come to expect more from the charabanc, and in the years between 1920 and 1930, major improvements were made to the design of the vehicles, which resulted in covered tops, upholstered seating and proper windows. By the 1920s, day excursions to the seaside were being offered, and the old-fashioned charabanc developed into the luxury motor coach.

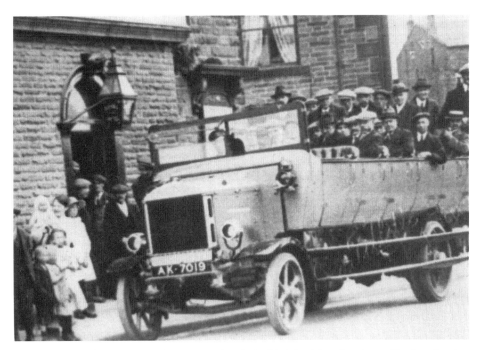

Setting out on what appears to be a men-only trip is this Maudslay charabanc. The location is thought to be Crossflatts, near Bingley, but the date is not known. (*Author's collection*)

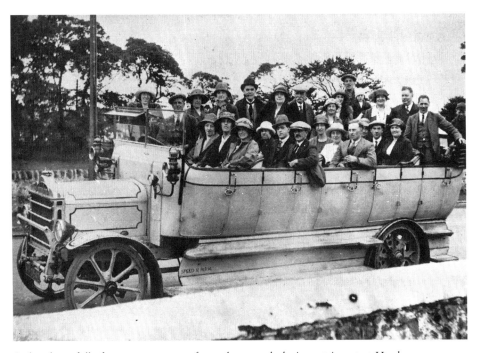

A charabanc full of passengers pauses for a photograph during a trip out at Harden, near Bingley, possibly on its way to the Goit Stock Waterfalls. The owner of the vehicle is not known. (*Bradford Libraries*)

CHAPTER SIX

Corporation Motor Buses 1926-74

Bradford Corporation was the last of the local municipal operators to introduce motor buses. Leeds was the first in 1906, followed by Todmorden (1907), Keighley (1908), Halifax (1912) and Huddersfield (1920). However, it took Bradford until May 1926 before the first route was introduced between Bankfoot and Lister Park. Despite this slow start they soon made up for lost time with additional routes to Haworth Road, Cutler Heights, Bierley and Fagley in the same year.

The routes opened in 1927 were largely peripheral ones, while in 1928, Greengates and Tyersal received their first motor buses. A through route to Leeds also opened in 1928 as did one to Huddersfield in 1929.

The earliest motor buses were a mixture of AEC, Leyland Lion and Bristol B-type single deckers, while towards the end of 1928, a batch of Leyland Titan double deckers with open rear staircases arrived, most of which remained in service until the late 1940s. More sophisticated vehicles of AEC and Daimler manufacture entered service during the 1930s.

A number of tram routes were converted to motor bus operation including Drighlington (1933) and Shelf and Undercliffe (1935). The outbreak of war in 1939 brought a halt to the tramway conversion programme, and utility Guy and Daimler double deckers with wooden seats were allocated to the Corporation by the Ministry of War Transport.

After the war, Daimler, Leyland, Crossley and AEC double deckers entered service in large numbers, and many new motor bus routes were introduced as a result of the replacement of tram routes, notably to West Bowling (1947), Queensbury (1949) and Odsal (1950). Services to new housing estates began to Buttershaw (1950), Thorpe Edge (1953), Woodside (1956) and Holme Wood (1958).

The City Circle route commenced in 1954 and proved very popular both as a way of seeing the city as well as serving the outer suburbs. The year 1958 saw the acquisition of twenty-five former London Transport buses, which replaced the last of the wartime utility vehicles. In marked contrast, the first of the city's front-entrance buses entered service the following year.

The conversion of trolleybus routes to motor bus operation began in 1962 and was completed in 1972. Large quantities of front-entrance AEC Regent Vs entered service until 1966 when a change in buying policy saw a return to Daimlers and Leylands. The first rear-engined buses arrived in 1967 and were Leyland Atlanteans, though Daimler Fleetlines also became popular.

Bradford and Leeds buses jointly took over the Bradford to Leeds via Pudsey route of independent operator Samuel Ledgard in October 1967, taking the Corporation's buses to some previously unfamiliar locations. Another takeover, this time on 1 March 1971, saw Bradford's buses reaching Halifax on the two routes previously operated by Hebble Motor Services.

In post-war years, only twelve single deckers were purchased, and little work was found for them; they became almost forgotten members of the fleet. They comprised two AEC Reliances of 1958, and five AEC Swifts and five Leyland Panthers in 1969.

One-man-operated buses began in Bradford on 31 December 1972. Plans were being prepared for the formation of the new West Yorkshire Passenger Transport Executive, and Bradford's famous blue buses became part of history at midnight on 31 March 1974.

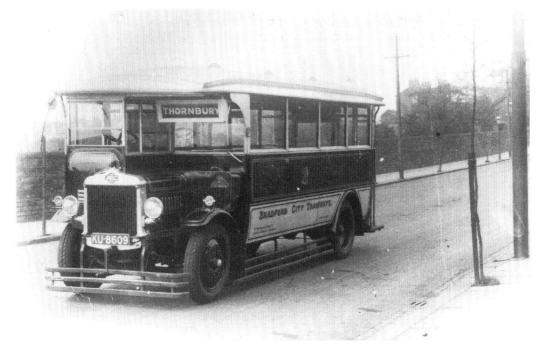

One of Bradford's first motor buses, no. 309, a 1926 AEC 413 with bodywork by United Automobile Services, in Killinghall Road. (*Author's collection*)

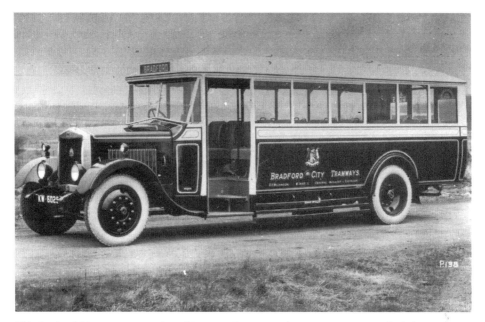

This Leyland Lioness was purchased in 1929 for use on the service to Tong, which began in 1927. It was later converted into an illuminated vehicle, and we shall see this vehicle again in yet another guise in chapter ten. (*Author's collection*)

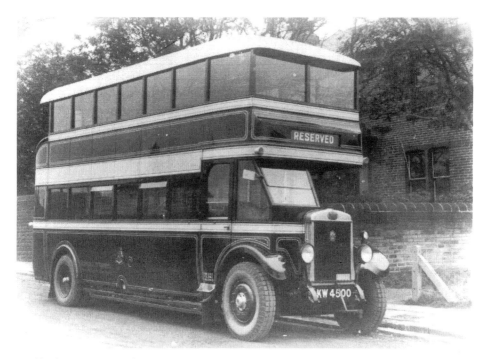

Bradford Corporation's first double-deck motor buses were fifteen Leyland Titan TD1s with Leyland bodywork, purchased in 1928. Here is no. 353, the first of the batch seen when new. It ran in service until 1946. (*Author's collection*)

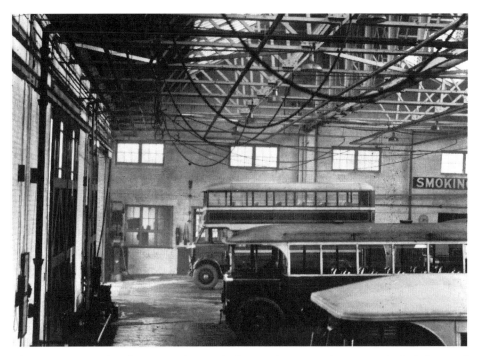

This interior view of Ludlam Street depot, which opened in 1932, shows two single deckers and one of the Leyland TD1s. (*Bradford Libraries*)

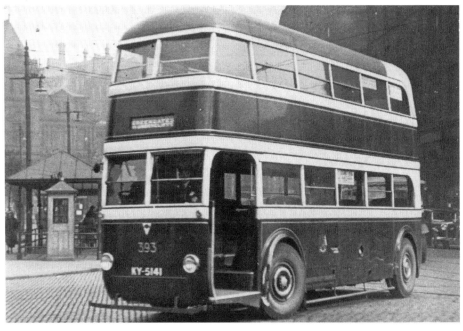

Front-entrance buses are not new. In 1933, the Corporation purchased this solitary AEC Q-type double decker, which is seen here in Forster Square on the Greengates via Undercliffe service. It only ran until 1939 and was then sold. (*Author's collection*)

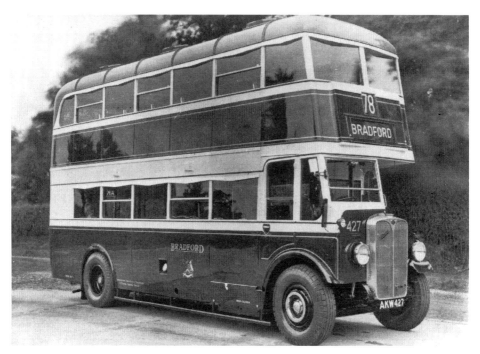

Before the Second World War, the Corporation purchased AEC, Leyland and Daimler double deckers. Here is AEC Regent no. 427, which had an English Electric body, and ran in service in Bradford from 1936 to 1949. (*Author's collection*)

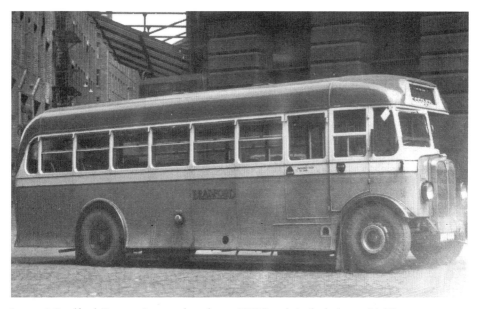

In 1936, Bradford Corporation purchased two AEC Regal single deckers with Weymann bodywork. Although they were rarely used in service, they lasted until 1957. No. 444 is seen here outside the former General Post Office in Forster Square. (*Roy Marshall, Omnibus Society*)

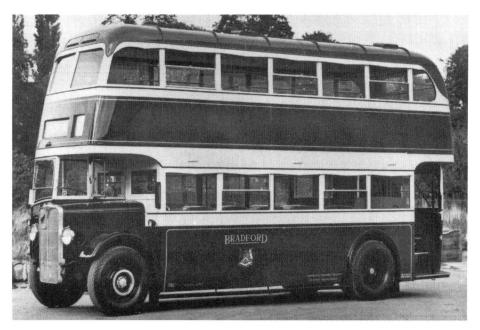

New in 1938 as an AEC demonstrator, this attractive Weymann-bodied Regent was purchased by Bradford in 1940 and became no.466 in the fleet. It only ran in the city for ten years before it was sold. (*Roy Marshall, Omnibus Society*)

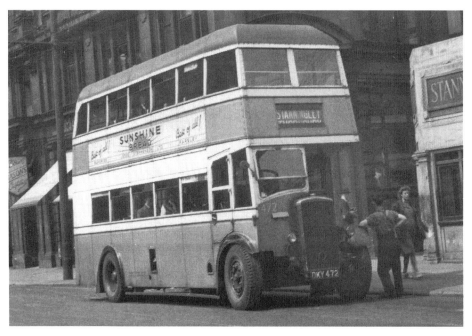

The wartime utility buses may have been rugged and uncomfortable, but they had a certain attraction. Seen here in Hall Ings about to depart for Stanningley is Massey-bodied Daimler CWG5 no. 472, dating from June 1943. It was in service in Bradford until 1953. (*Roy Marshall, Omnibus Society*)

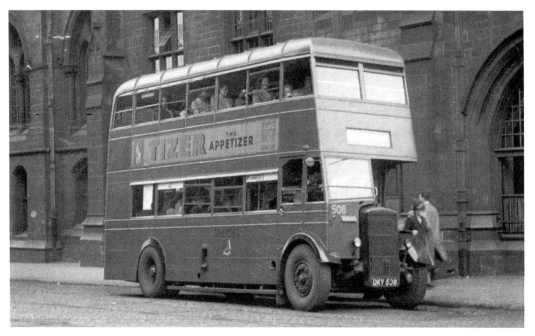

During the war years, the majority of new double deckers were Daimlers with utility bodywork. This early post-war view shows no. 508 loading outside the Town Hall for a trip to Wyke. Its Duple bodywork is still in wartime livery. (*Roy Marshall, Omnibus Society*)

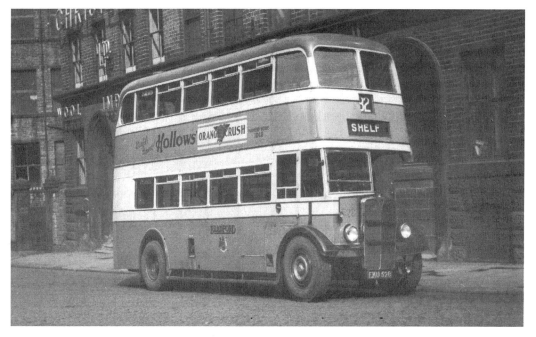

In 1947-48, twenty AEC Regent IIIs, with relatively rare Northern Coachbuilders bodywork, were purchased by Bradford. Seen here when new, no. 528 is about to set off for Shelf. (*Roy Marshall, Omnibus Society*)

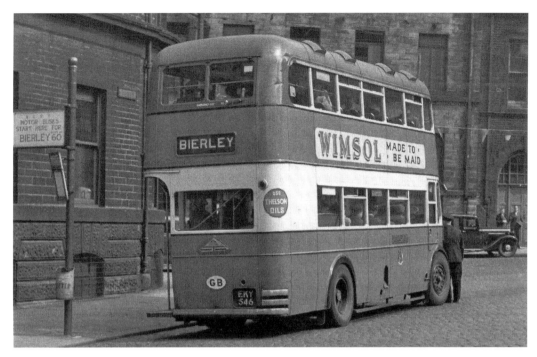

Brush-bodied Daimler no. 546 took part in a 'British Week' trade fair in Copenhagen when new in 1948 and carried a GB plate on the back panel as a result. It is seen here at work on the Bierley route. (*R. F. Mack*)

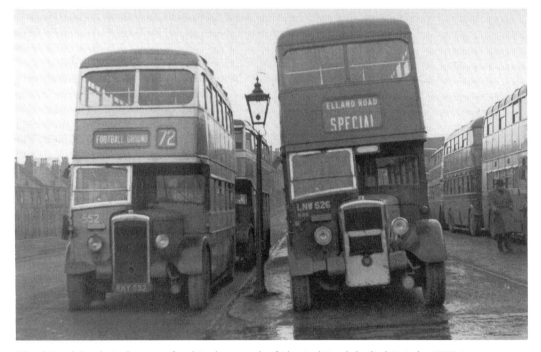

Elland Road, Leeds, is the venue for this photograph of identical Brush-bodied Daimler CVD6s: Bradford no. 552 and Leeds no. 526. (*R. F. Mack*)

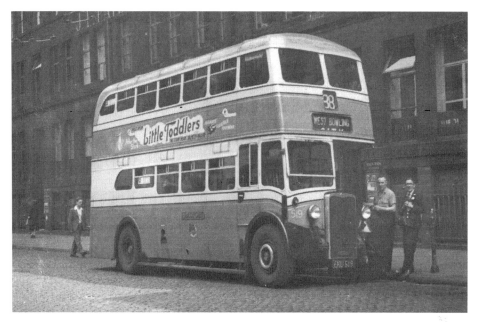

In 1948, the Corporation purchased six Crossley double deckers numbered 518-23. They were underpowered vehicles and spent most of their lives on the West Bowling route. They were withdrawn and sold for scrap ten years later. (*Roy Marshall, Omnibus Society*)

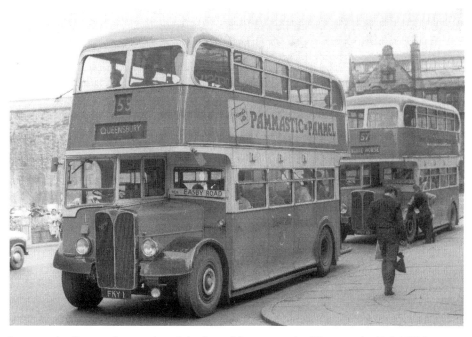

In 1949, the Corporation purchased the first of forty attractive Weymann-bodied AEC Regent IIIs. Seen here in Town Hall Street are the first of the batch, no. 1 and no. 10, both working on the Great Horton Road services, with which they were associated for many years. (*Author's collection*)

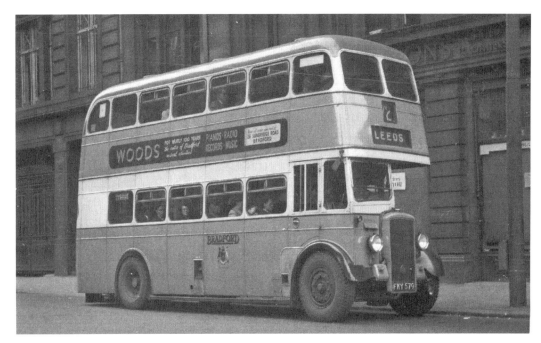

Unusual purchases in 1950 were six Daimler CVD6s with rare Barnard of Norwich bodywork. They were used on the 72 route to Leeds, on which 7 ft 6 in wide vehicles were required. No. 579 is seen here in Hall Ings prior to its departure for Leeds. (*Roy Marshall, Omnibus Society*)

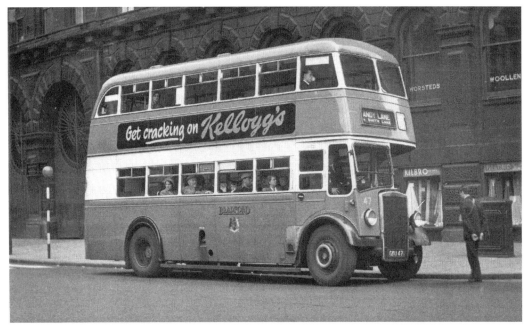

After the war, Bradford bought forty-five Leyland Titan PD2/3s with Leyland bodywork, in two batches. Representing the second batch is no. 47, dating from 1950, seen here in Forster Square on its way to Sandy Lane. What has attracted the conductor's attention? (*Roy Marshall, Omnibus Society*)

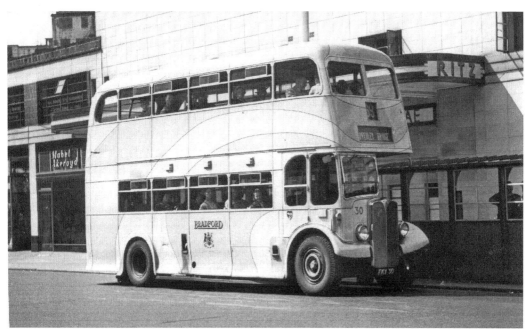

For the coronation in 1953, the Corporation painted a number of buses in special liveries. Here is AEC Regent III no. 30, outside the Ritz Cinema, on its way to Apperley Bridge. (*Roy Marshall, Omnibus Society*)

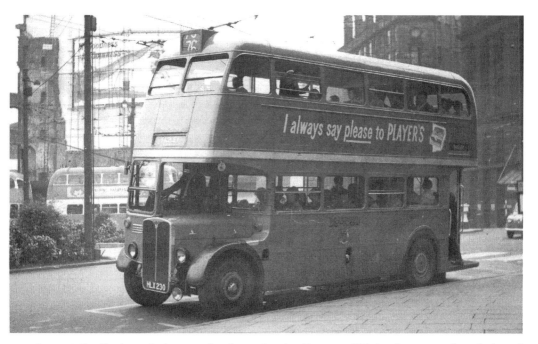

In 1958, Bradford acquired twenty-five former London Transport RT-class buses to replace the last of its wartime utility buses. They were given a quick coat of blue paint, which looked darker on top of London's red. Here no. 416 waits in Forster Square on its way from Wrose to Fagley. (*Roy Marshall, Omnibus Society*)

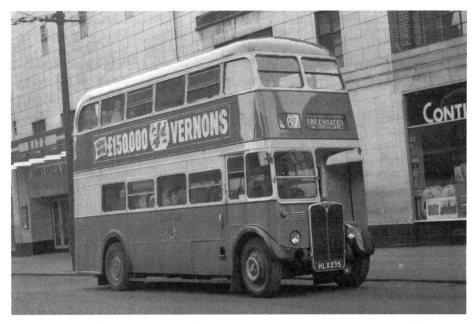

When the London buses were repainted in traditional Corporation colours they looked more like proper Bradford buses. Here is no. 421, with less-common Saunders-Roe bodywork, outside the Ritz Cinema on its way to Greengates via Undercliffe. Note the revised destination indicator layout. (*Roy Marshall, Omnibus Society*)

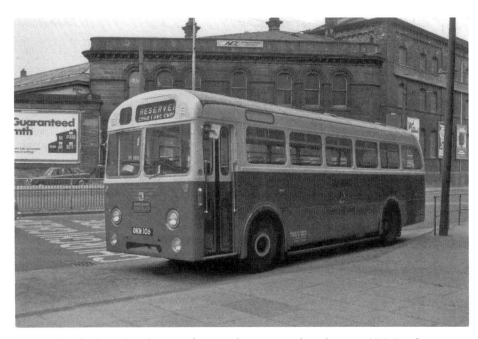

In 1958, Bradford purchased a pair of AEC Reliances to replace the 1936 AEC Regals. Originally numbered 301-2, they were later re-numbered 501-2. No. 501 is seen here parked in Canal Road. (*Author's collection*)

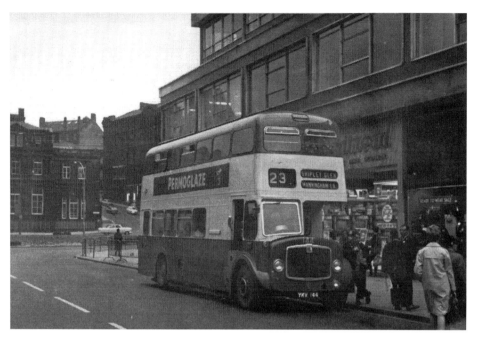

Three AEC Regent Vs were repainted in 1966 in this experimental livery incorporating a larger area of cream than normal. The idea was not pursued. Here, no. 144 of 1963 stands in Cheapside on its way from Bradford Moor to Shipley Glen in August of that year. (*D. Akrigg*)

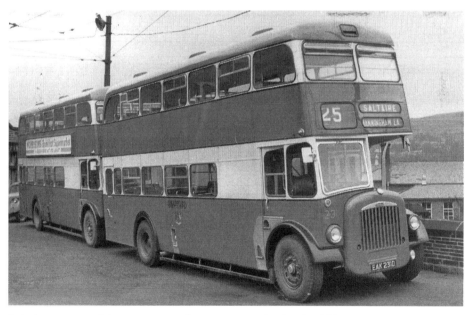

Daimlers re-entered the Corporation fleet in 1966 with a batch of fifteen forward-entrance double deckers with bodywork by Neepsend of Sheffield. They were normally used on the Bradford Moor–Crossflatts route and no. 231 is seen here on the forecourt of Saltaire depot. (*Author's collection*)

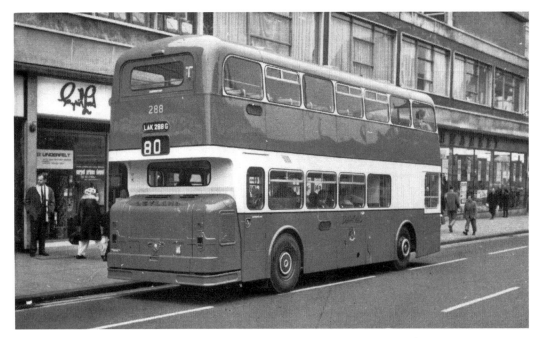

Bradford's first rear-engined buses were purchased in 1967. This scene in Petergate shows 1968 Leyland Atlantean no. 288 on route 80 to Bankfoot via Heaton. (*Author's collection*)

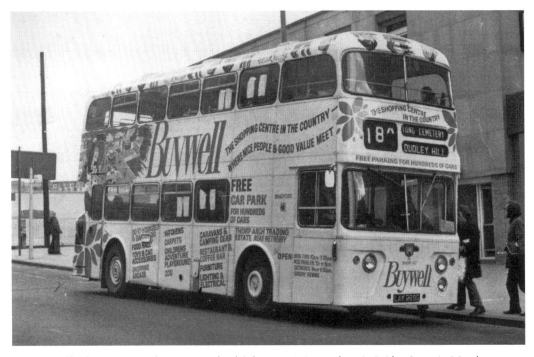

This is Bradford no. 289, another 1968 Leyland Atlantean. It is seen here in Bridge Street in March 1974 in an advertising livery for Buywell Discount Stores. Route 18 was formerly a trolleybus route. (*D. Akrigg*)

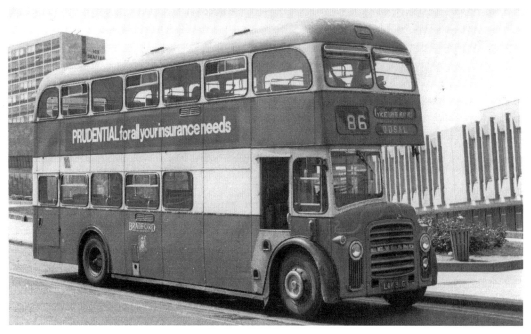

Fifteen of these Alexander-bodied Leyland PD3s were purchased by Bradford in 1969. No. 311 (2311 in the PTE fleet) stands in Hall Ings on route 86 to Wyke. These were among the author's favourite buses. Fortunately, sister vehicle no. 309 is preserved. (*Author's collection*)

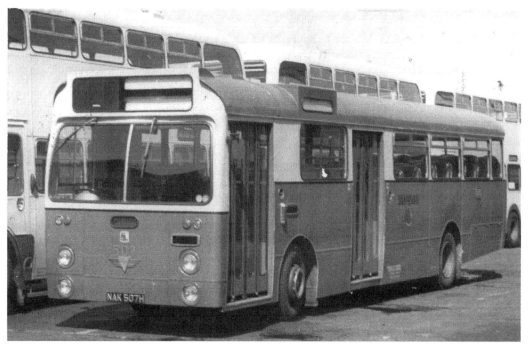

In 1969, Bradford purchased ten new single deckers comprising five AEC Swifts and five Leyland Panthers. Here is AEC Swift no. 507 on a private hire trip at Blackpool. (*Author's collection*)

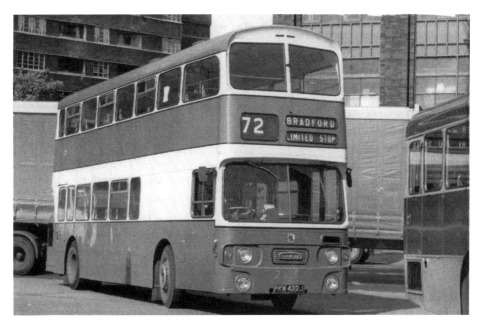

In 1970-71, Bradford took delivery of seventy of these Alexander-bodied vehicles – forty on Daimler Fleetline and thirty on Leyland Atlantean chassis. Fleetline 422 (now 2422) is seen entering Leeds Central bus station on route 72 with the blind already changed for the return journey. Behind, to the left, are the former Quarry Hill flats, now the site of the BBC studios. (*Author's collection*)

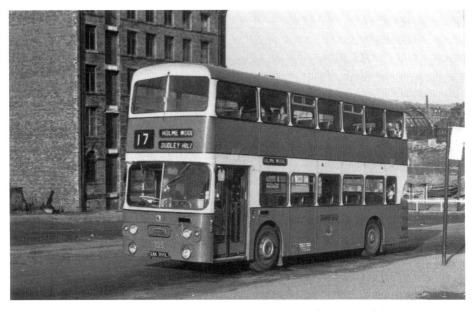

The very last new bus to be purchased by Bradford prior to the formation of the West Yorkshire Passenger Transport Executive in April 1974 was this Alexander-bodied Daimler Fleetline, no. 355, which is seen here in Croft Street. (*Author's collection*)

CHAPTER SEVEN

Other Motor Buses to 1974

Bradford is credited with having what may well have been the first motor bus route in the country. This took place in 1897 when for a short time Mr James Edward Tuke ran a small Daimler bus between the Town Hall and Four Lane Ends. In 1900, the same vehicle appeared on a short-lived route along Manningham Lane run by Mr Albert House.

In the 1920s, there were numerous small businesses running buses into Bradford, notably the Brigg Brothers of Wilsden, the Calder Bus Company of Bailiff Bridge, the Premier Transport Company of Keighley, Edwin Box of Batley, G. H. Kilburn of Heckmondwike, Bullocks of Featherstone, and Robinson's 'Hedna Bus Service' of Eccleshill. Within a few years, most of these would be taken over by larger companies, and it is the larger concerns that people tend to recall the most. Probably the best known of these was the West Yorkshire Road Car Company. Formed in January 1928 by an amalgamation of the Harrogate & District Road Car Company and Blythe & Berwick Ltd of Bradford, its red buses were a familiar sight on Bradford's streets for the next sixty years. Frequent services along Manningham Lane ran to Keighley, Skipton, Shipley, Baildon, Otley, Ilkley and Harrogate.

Hebble Motor Services began operating into Bradford from Halifax as a result of the General Strike of 1926. Two routes were operated, one via Shelf, the other via Queensbury. They also ran from Bradford to Huddersfield, and on a local route to Wibsey and Buttershaw.

The Yorkshire Woollen District Transport Company of Dewsbury began services into Bradford in 1926, as did the West Riding Automobile Company of Wakefield. The Yorkshire Traction Company of Barnsley ran a service from Bradford to Barnsley, and from 1932 this was extended to Sheffield and was worked jointly with Yorkshire Woollen and the Sheffield Joint Omnibus Committee which resulted in the occasional sighting of a Sheffield bus in Bradford.

The well-known Leeds-based operator Samuel Ledgard began operating a route from Leeds to Bradford via Pudsey in 1926.

Long-distance services developed during the 1920s. One of the earliest was Doncaster-based Bentinck & Ensign Motor Services, which developed a service between Bradford and London via Leeds, Doncaster, Nottingham, Leicester and Northampton. West Yorkshire began services to Morecambe in 1928 (jointly with Ribble Motor Services from 1932) and to Blackpool and Scarborough at around the same time. A service between Newcastle and Liverpool via Leeds and Bradford was begun in 1930 by Tyne and Mersey Motor Services Ltd, and most of these services are still operated today, though by different companies.

Chester Street bus station was used by the West Yorkshire Road Car Company, Hebble Motor Services, the Yorkshire Woollen District Transport Company, and Samuel Ledgard, plus long-distance coach services. Hebble and Yorkshire Woollen also used Nelson Street while West Riding used Union Street.

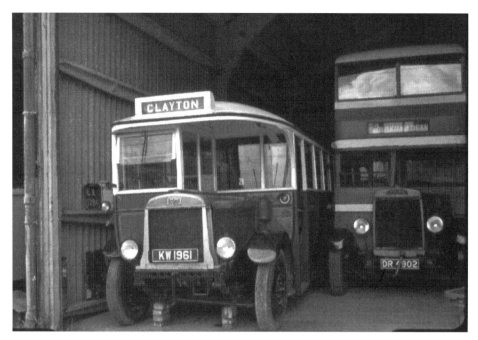

This 1927 Leyland-bodied Leyland Lion was new to Blythe & Berwick of Bradford and ran on the Clayton route. The firm was acquired by West Yorkshire in January 1928 and the vehicle survives to this day at the East Anglia Transport Museum at Carlton Colville, near Lowestoft. (*Author's collection*)

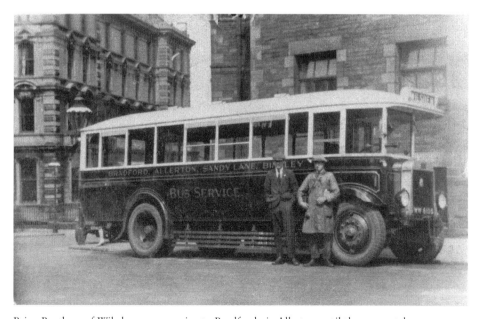

Brigg Brothers of Wilsden ran a service to Bradford via Allerton until they were taken over by Hebble Motor Services in May 1928. Leyland Lion WW 6105 is seen here at the Bradford terminus in Great Horton Road. (*Author's collection*)

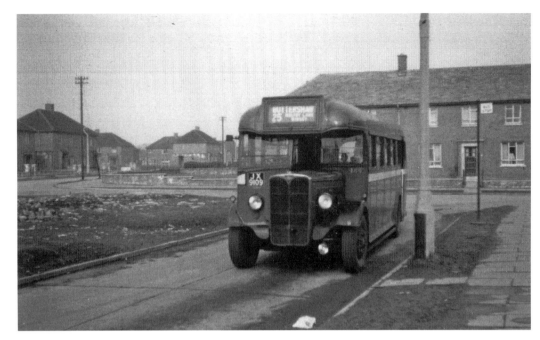

Hebble operated the short no. 25 route from Chester Street bus station to the Buttershaw estate where Weymann-bodied AEC Regal no. 184 is seen. It is still painted in the red and cream livery with dark-brown roof. (*Author's collection*)

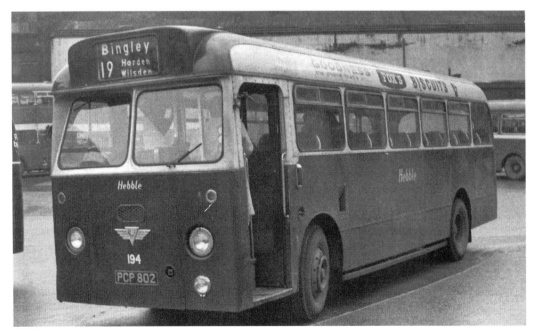

Hebble's Alexander-bodied AEC Reliance no. 194 of 1962 is seen at Chester Street bus station ready to depart on the rural route to Bingley via Wilsden and Harden, which was taken over from Brigg of Wilsden in 1928. (*D. Akrigg*)

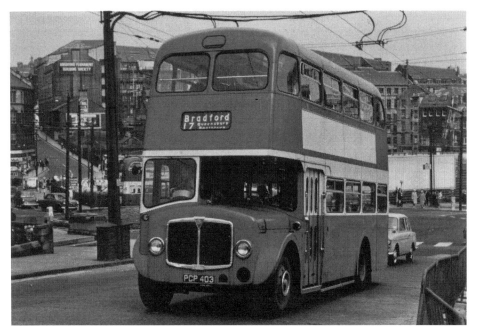

New the same year as the Reliance in the previous picture, AEC Regent V PCP 403 is starting the climb up Little Horton Lane towards Chester Street bus station at the end of its journey from Halifax on route 17. (*Author's collection*)

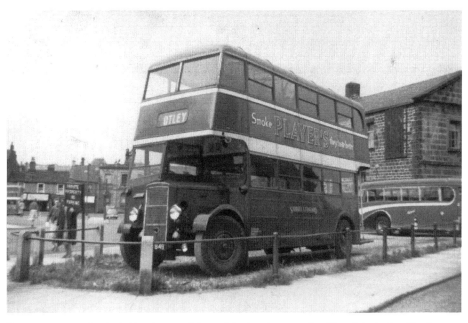

For many years, the dark-blue buses of Samuel Ledgard were a familiar sight in Bradford on routes to Harrogate via Otley and Leeds via Pudsey. The firm sold out to West Yorkshire in 1967. Here, a former London Transport utility Daimler rests between trips in Otley bus station. (*Author's collection*)

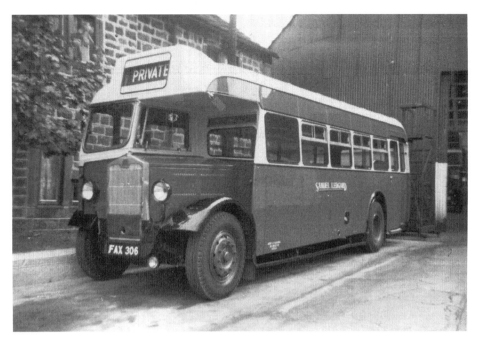

Between 1959 and 1962, Ledgard used five Albion CX13s with rare Brislington Body Works bodies on the service between Bradford and Harrogate. Seen outside its Otley depot around 1960 is FAX 306. (*Author's collection*)

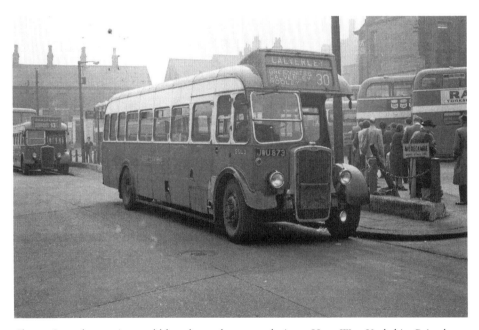

Chester Street bus station could be a busy place at peak times. Here, West Yorkshire Bristol LL5G SGL 3 of 1950 is parked up prior to departing on a short-working of the no. 30 Leeds service to Calverley. To the right, a small group of people anxiously await their bus. (*Author's collection*)

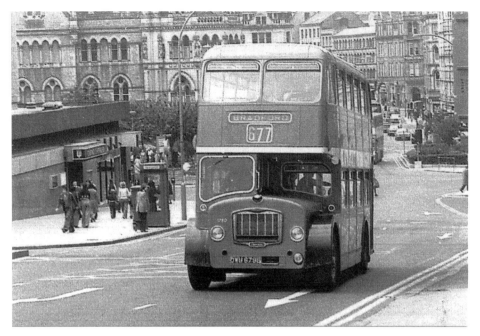

Approaching the Interchange at the end of its journey from Shipley on route 677 is West Yorkshire's 1780, a Bristol FS6B new in 1964 as DX 180. This is one part of Bradford city centre that has not changed in recent years. (*Author's collection*)

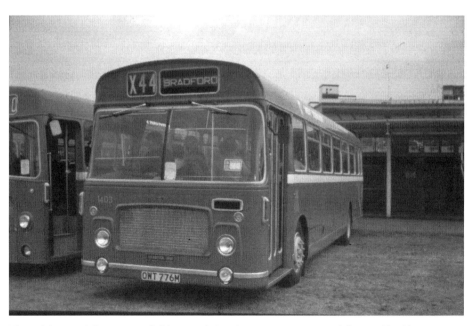

The red buses of the West Yorkshire Road Car Company were part of the Bradford bus scene from 1928 to 1998. Here, one of the company's many Bristol REs with Eastern Coach Works bodywork is seen at York Racecourse at a rally of preserved vehicles. (*Author's collection*)

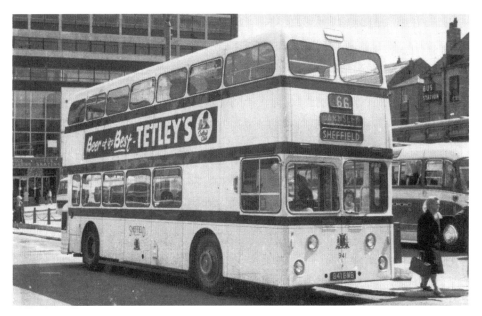

For many years there was an hourly service between Bradford and Sheffield via Barnsley. It was operated jointly by Yorkshire Woollen, Yorkshire Traction and the Sheffield Joint Omnibus Committee. Seen here in Chester Street bus station in July 1967 is Sheffield Leyland Atlantean no. 941 about to depart for its home city on a journey that would take just less than three hours. (*D. Akrigg*)

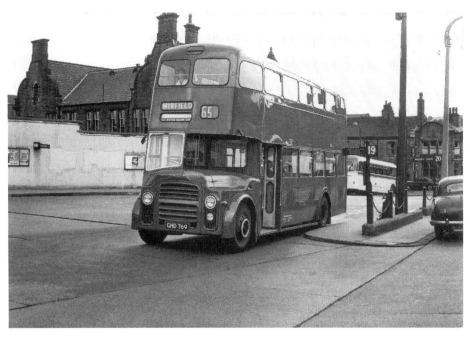

A quiet day in Chester Street bus station sees Yorkshire Woollen Leyland Titan PD3 no. 897 of 1962 awaiting passengers for a journey to Mirfield on route 65. Perhaps it was a Sunday? (*Author's collection*)

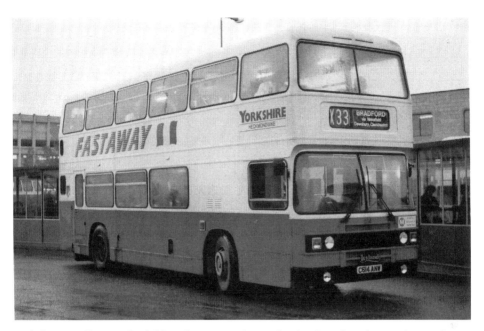

Yorkshire Woollen's Leyland Olympian no. 614 is seen leaving Dewsbury bus station on the last leg of the journey from Sheffield to Bradford on the X33. It wears a special variation of the traditional red and cream livery. (*Author's collection*)

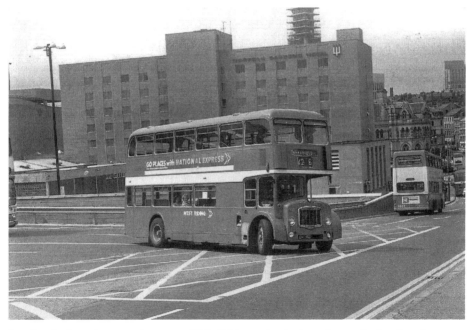

Leaving the Interchange on its way to Wakefield on what looks to be a quiet Sunday afternoon is West Riding 535, a former Bristol Omnibus Bristol FLF6G that was one of twenty-seven purchased to replace the earlier, mechanically troublesome, Guy Wulfrunians. (*Author's collection*)

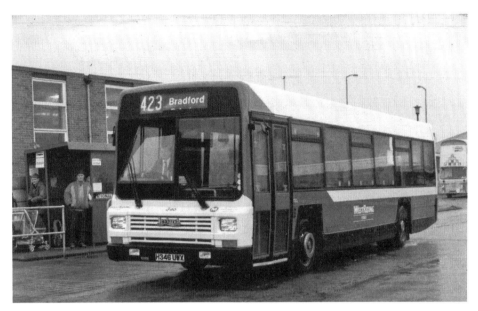

West Riding's green and cream buses were regular visitors to Bradford on the services to Wakefield that were taken over from Bullock's of Featherstone in 1950. Leyland Lynx no. 364 prepares to leave the Saville Street depot in Wakefield for a trip to Bradford. (*Author's collection*)

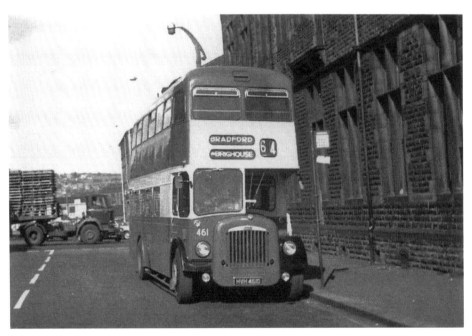

Huddersfield Corporation Daimler CVG6LX/30 no. 461, with East Lancashire bodywork, stands in Lord Street in its home town prior to departing on route 64 to Bradford, which was jointly worked by Bradford, Huddersfield and Hebble Motor Services from 1927 to 1970. (*Author's collection*)

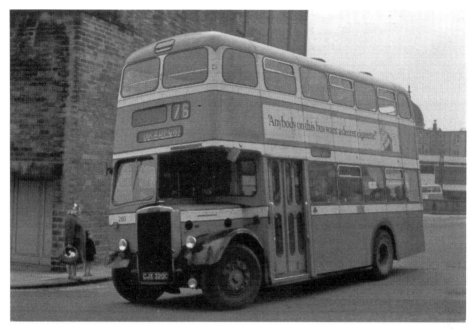

Departing from the old bus station in Halifax is Halifax Corporation's no. 280, a Leyland PD2/37 with Weymann bodywork, new in 1965. Route 76 to Bradford via Queensbury was the forerunner of today's route 576, operated by First. (*Author's collection*)

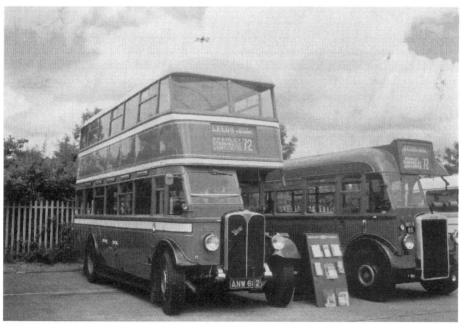

Not many people will remember when Leeds motor buses were once blue, though a different shade to Bradford's. Here, two restored Leeds buses, including AEC Regent no. 139 of 1934 on the left are pretending to be on route 72 from Bradford. (*Author's collection*)

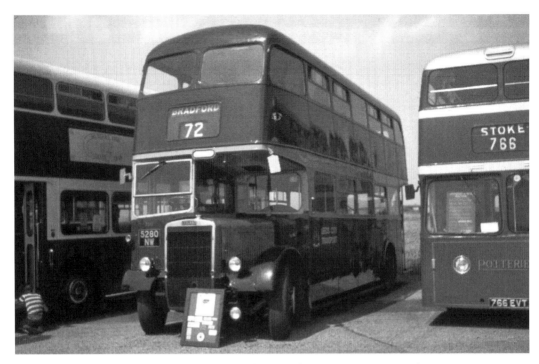

This is the way most people will remember Leeds buses in the smart two-tone green livery. Here, Leyland PD3 no. 280 of 1959 is seen at the Sandtoft Trolleybus Museum in July 1984 as if it is just about to depart for Bradford on route 72. (*Author's collection*)

CHAPTER EIGHT

Buses Since 1974

On 1 April 1974, the West Yorkshire Passenger Transport Executive (Metro) came into being, amalgamating the municipal bus fleets of Bradford, Leeds, Halifax, Huddersfield and Todmorden into one organisation. A new, rather insipid livery of Verona Green and Buttermilk was introduced, replacing the former municipal colours. In May 1976, a county-wide route renumbering scheme was implemented, as a result of which the majority of Bradford's bus routes received numbers in the 600s.

A major milestone in public transport was the opening of Bradford's new Transport Interchange on 27 March 1977, bringing bus, coach and train services together. Since that time, the bus station part of the site has been rebuilt several times, and is now much smaller than when it was originally built. The former Chester Street bus station, which was used by out-of-town services, closed at the same time.

In October 1986, bus services in Britain were deregulated in order to open the market up to competition. One result of this was that the Passenger Transport Executive was no longer permitted to operate actual bus services and so the services and buses came under a separate company – Yorkshire Rider Ltd. A much more attractive livery of dark green and primrose was introduced as a result. Bradford saw very little in the way of competition on bus services compared to some places, and it was to take a while before new operators came on the scene. Three notable ones were Black Prince of Morley (1992-2005), Blue Bus of Horwich (1996) and the Bradford Bus Company (2001-03).

In August 1998, the familiar red and cream buses of the West Yorkshire Road Car Company in Bradford and Leeds were taken over by Yorkshire Rider. The Keighley–Bradford route became part of the new Keighley & District Travel.

The year 1995 saw the merger of Yorkshire Rider Ltd with the Badgerline Group to form a new company called First Bus. In September that year the Bradford fleet adopted the name Bradford Traveller, and a new blue and red livery was adopted.

The red buses of the Yorkshire Woollen District Transport Company and the green ones of the West Riding Automobile Company became part of the new

Arriva organisation and their new corporate colours of Aquamarine and Cotswold Stone were gradually adopted.

During 2000, First Bus introduced its new corporate livery of white, purple and pink, and Bradford's buses changed colour yet again.

The Manchester Road guided busway was opened in January 2002, complete with some very futuristic-looking bus shelters.

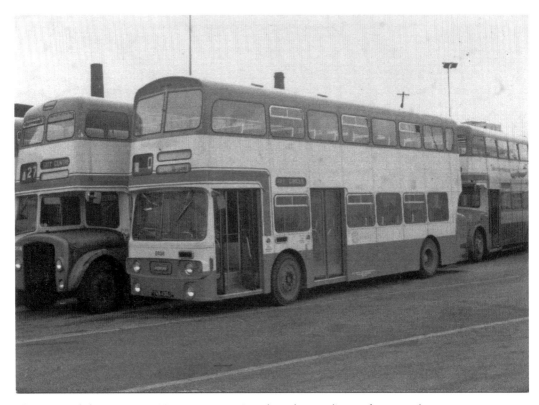

The West Yorkshire Passenger Transport Executive adopted a new livery of green and cream on its formation in April 1974. In this view, former Bradford 438, a 1970 Daimler Fleetline now renumbered 2438, stands in the yard at Ludlam Street depot. (*Author's collection*)

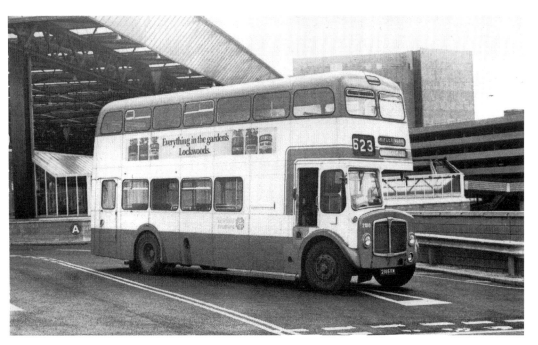

Former Bradford City Transport AEC Regent V no. 186, now renumbered 2186 in the West Yorkshire PTE fleet, departs from the Interchange on its way to Shipley Glen. The overall roof of the original Interchange can be seen. (*D. Akrigg*)

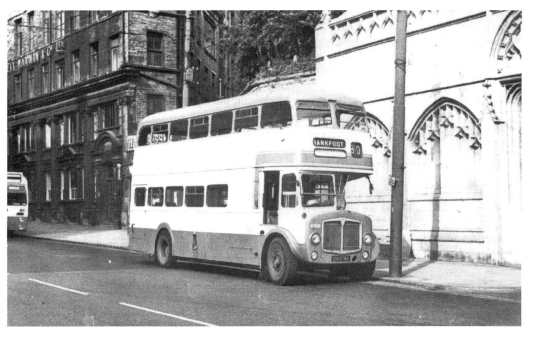

Following the formation of the PTE in April 1974, many buses were re-allocated to other districts including six Roe-bodied AEC Regent Vs, which came to Bradford from Huddersfield. Seen here is 4198 in the new livery at the bottom of Bolton Road. (*D. Akrigg*)

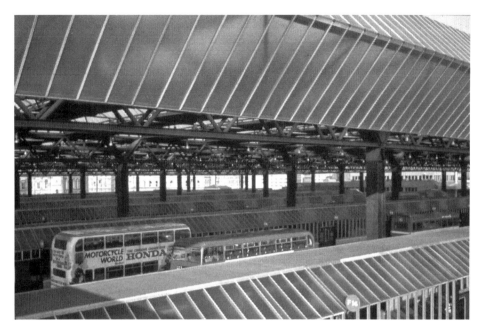

When the Interchange opened in 1977, it was much larger than it is today. This view shows the original extent of the site with its six platforms plus a number of West Yorkshire buses. (*Author's collection*)

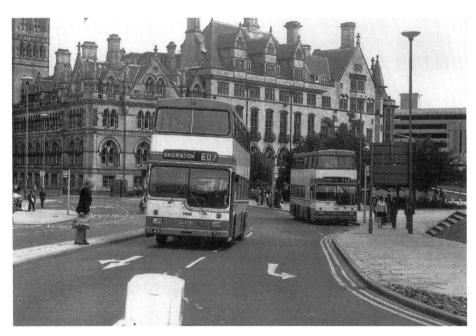

In 1975-76, the Bradford bus fleet received ninety-five Scania 'Metropolitans'. These fast, comfortable buses could be found on routes all over the city. Here, no. 2662 heads away from the City Hall on a trip to Thornton. The one in the lay-by appears to be lost as it is showing 'Central Bus Station 618'. (*Author's collection*)

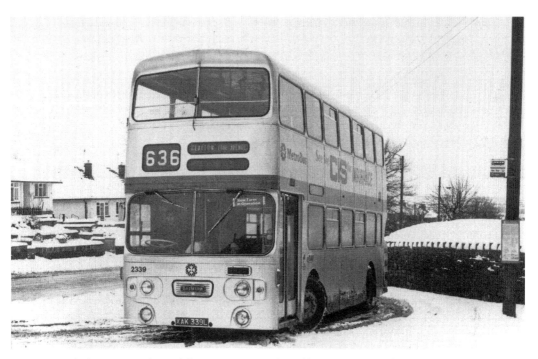

To mark the Queen's Silver Jubilee in 1977, a number of buses were painted in a special silver livery with a purple band. Daimler Fleetline no. 2339 is seen here at Clayton in wintry conditions. (*D. Akrigg*)

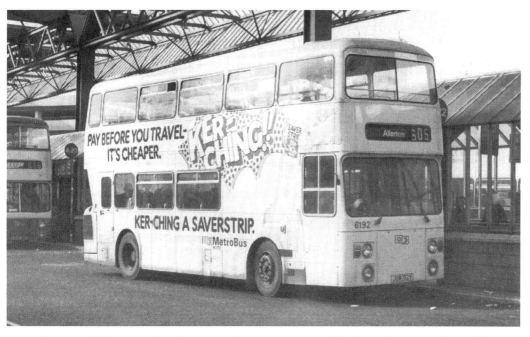

Cheaper multi-journey tickets known as Saverstrips were introduced in July 1983 and several buses, including Leyland Atlantean no. 6192 seen here in the Interchange, were repainted in this special white livery to advertise the new tickets. (*D. Akrigg*)

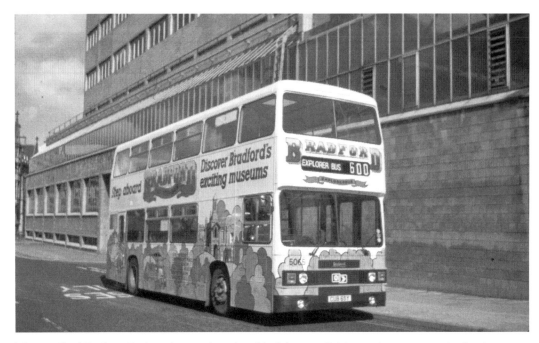

The 'Bradford Explorer Bus' service was introduced in July 1984 linking various museums in the city, and was operated by this special-liveried Leyland Olympian, no. 5065. The service was withdrawn at the end of the 1988 summer season. (*Author's collection*)

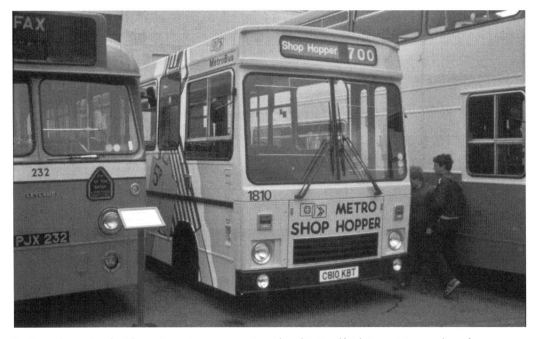

In December 1985, the 'Shop Hopper' service was introduced in Bradford. In 1986, a number of Optare-bodied Leyland Cubs were introduced on the route, though their use was short-lived. No. 1810, seen here, is now in preservation. (*Author's collection*)

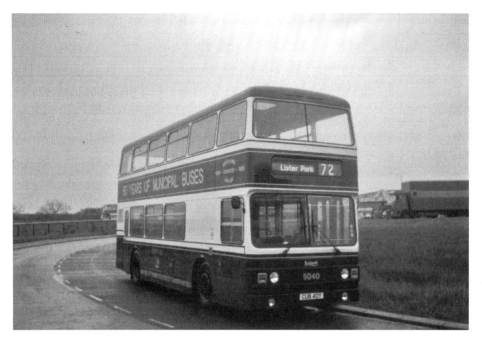

In 1986, this Leyland Olympian was repainted in the original Bradford colour scheme to celebrate the sixtieth anniversary of the introduction of municipal motor buses in the city. It was photographed at a special event at the Leyland works near Preston. (*Author's collection*)

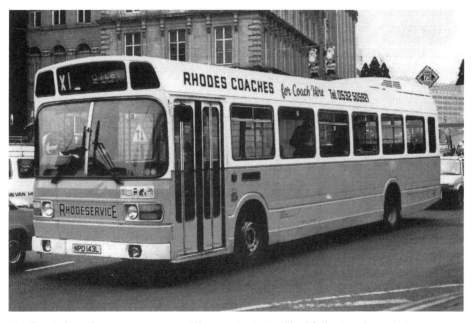

The first independent operator to provide a service in Bradford following deregulation was Rhodes Coaches of Yeadon who began service X1 to Otley via Leeds Bradford Airport in 1987. The company sold out to Yorkshire Rider in 1994. Leyland National NPD 143L is seen here in Hall Ings. (*Author's collection*)

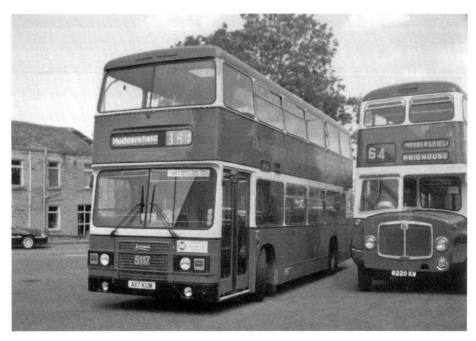

Leyland Olympian 5117 was repainted into the post-war Bradford livery in November 1991 and is seen here alongside preserved Bradford AEC Regent V no. 220 outside the former Ludlam Street depot. (*Author's collection*)

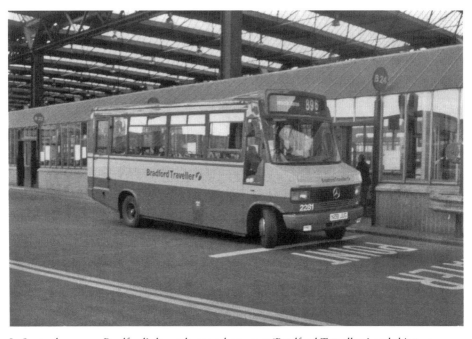

In September 1995, Bradford's buses became known as 'Bradford Travellers' and this two-tone blue livery was introduced. Mercedes-Benz minibus 2281 is seen here in the Interchange working on route 896 to Ravenscliffe Avenue. (*Author's collection*)

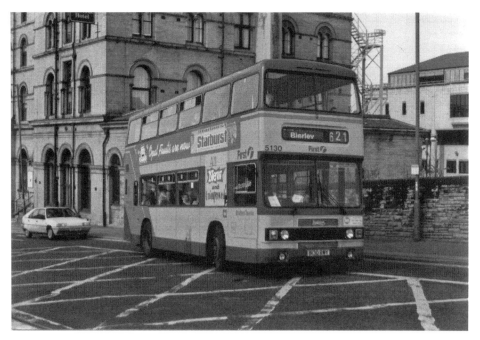

First Bradford Leyland Olympian no. 5130 displays the unusual blue and red livery applied to double deckers in 1995. It is seen in Bridge Street on the cross-city service 621 from Haworth Road to Bierley. (*Author's collection*)

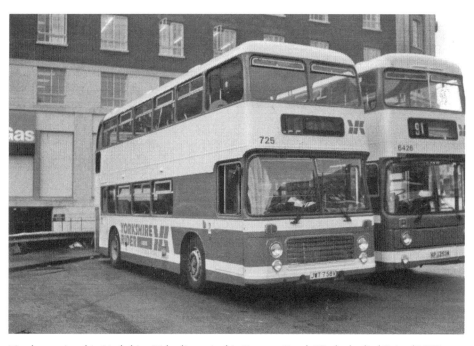

Newly repainted in Yorkshire Rider livery is this Eastern Coach Works-bodied Bristol VRT, seen in Leeds shortly before it was transferred to work in Bradford. (*Author's collection*)

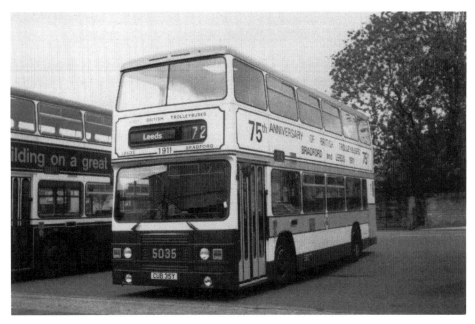

In 1986, Yorkshire Rider repainted two Leyland Olympians into special liveries to commemorate the opening of the Bradford and Leeds trolleybus systems in June 1911. This vehicle is in the original Leeds livery, while to the left is no. 5040 in the earlier Bradford dark-blue livery. (*Author's collection*)

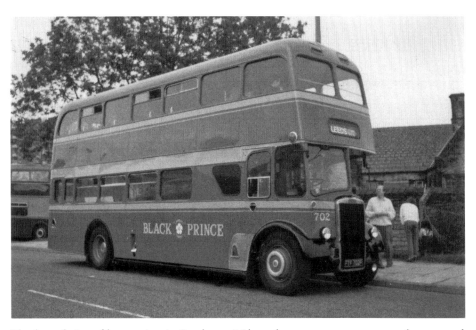

The deregulation of bus services in October 1986 brought many new operators to the streets of West Yorkshire. Black Prince of Morley ran between Bradford and Leeds via Pudsey from 1994 to 2005. This East Lancs-bodied Leyland PD3, FTF 702F, was typical of the smart condition in which this operator's vehicles were maintained. (*Author's collection*)

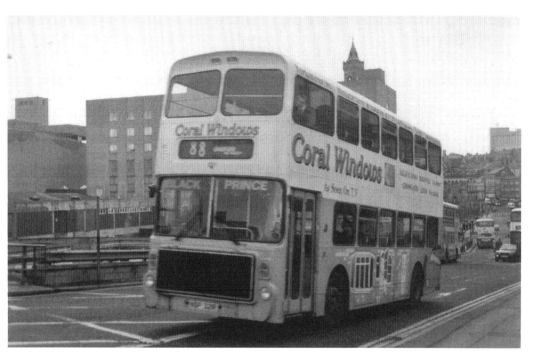

Many Black Prince vehicles carried overall advert liveries, including this former Tayside Volvo Ailsa, which is seen approaching Bradford Interchange. (*Author's collection*)

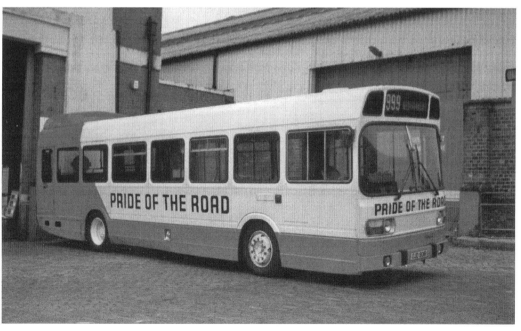

For some years after deregulation, Pride of the Road of Royston, near Barnsley ran a few local services in the Bradford area. Seen outside the former West Yorkshire Transport Museum is Leyland National OJD 901R, which was new to London Transport. (*Author's collection*)

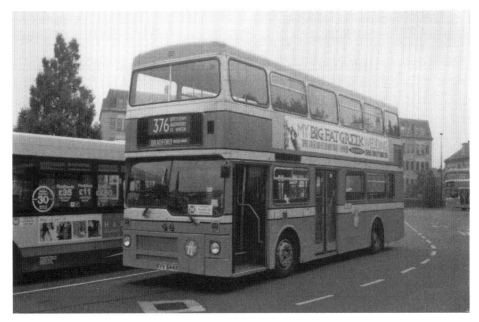

Another new operator on the local bus scene was the Halifax Joint Committee, which has run a number of services to Bradford. Here, a former London Transport MCW Metrobus stands in Halifax bus station prior to departing to Bradford on route 376, which no longer operates. (*Author's collection*)

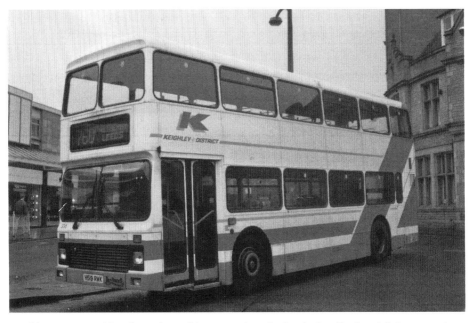

Keighley & District Travel was formed in 1989 when the Leeds, Bradford and Otley operations of West Yorkshire passed to Yorkshire Rider. Various liveries were tried over the years and this Northern Counties-bodied Leyland Olympian is seen in an early colour scheme in Keighley bus station. (*Author's collection*)

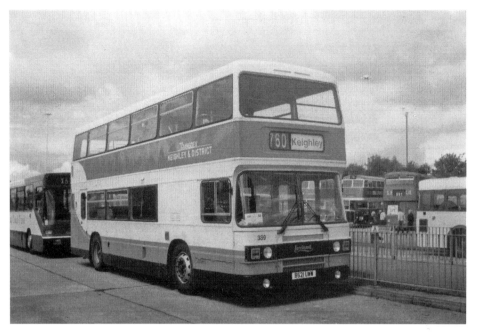

Keighley & District Travel later became part of the Transdev organisation. Eastern Coach Works-bodied Leyland Olympian no. 389 is seen in this attractive blue and white livery at a vintage vehicle rally in Leeds in 2009. (*Author's collection*)

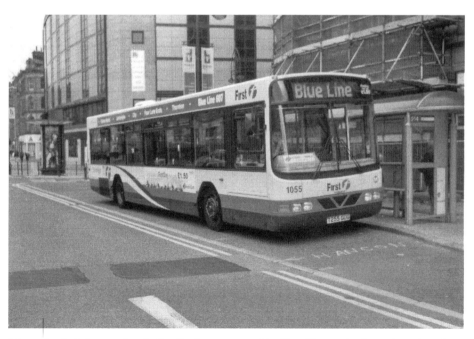

Most of today's bus services in Bradford are operated by First Group plc. A number of services are 'route-branded', and this low-floor Volvo operates on the 'Blue Line' route 607 between Thornton and Holme Wood. (*Author's collection*)

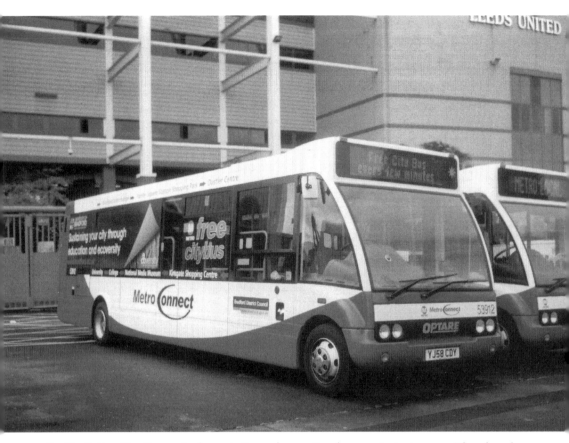

Bradford's Free City Bus service began in September 2008 and was an instant success. Three brand-new Optare Solo buses were provided by Metro for the service, one of which is seen here at an event in Leeds in 2009. (*Author's collection*)

CHAPTER NINE

Trams and Buses in the Streets

This section concentrates on street scenes as opposed to pictures of individual vehicles. Some of these show more than one form of transport, just like it used to be when trams, trolleybuses and motor buses ran alongside each other as part of an integrated transport network. Not only do they portray the various forms of transport in their true operating environment, but they show other aspects of life such as shop fronts and signs, period motor cars, people's fashions and styles of architecture, plus the hustle and bustle of a city at work. Suburban scenes were usually more tranquil, depicting a more leisurely pace of life. Old photographs often give the impression that life back then was sombre and depressing. Perhaps it was. I wonder what impression present-day photographs will give future historians?

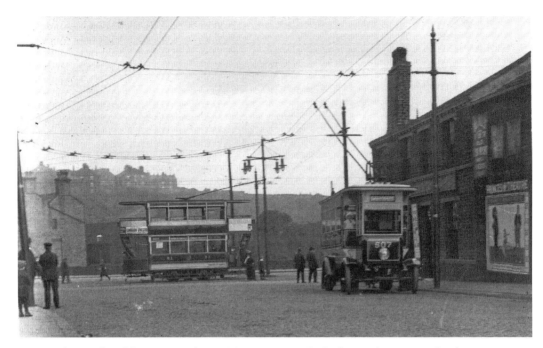

A tranquil view of Bankfoot in around 1914. Tram no. 81, in the background, appears to be almost empty. Trolleybus no. 507 is about to return to Laisterdyke, but what are the pedestrians waiting for? (*Author's collection*)

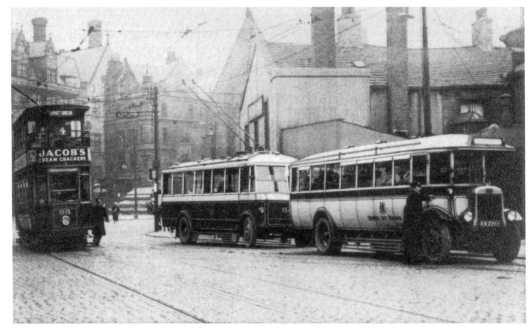

The end of Thornton Road with the Town Hall to the left. The motor bus is on the express service to Thornton, which only ran between May and September 1929. Tram no. 93 is on the Lidget Green service while the Leyland single deck trolleybus is bound for Clayton. (*Bradford Libraries*)

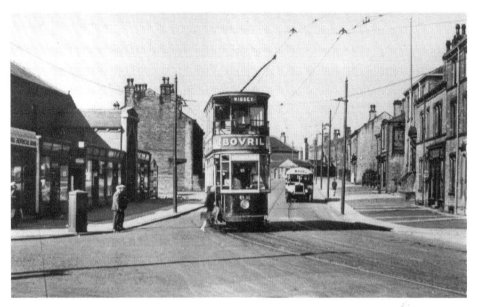

Fair Road, Wibsey, with tram no. 62 about to return to town. A Leyland Lion motor bus approaches on its way from Horton Bank Top to town. To the left of the tram is the Cosy Cinema, which was open from 1930 until 1961. (*Author's collection*)

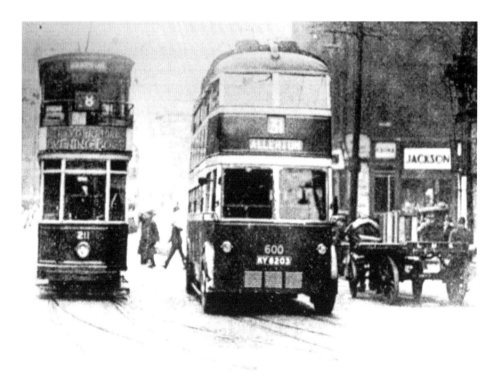

New AEC trolleybus no. 600 passes alongside tram no. 211 at the bottom of Sunbridge Road in 1934. The Allerton tram route was converted to trolleybus operation in 1929, and the Duckworth Lane trams would be replaced by trolleys in 1935. (*Bradford Libraries*)

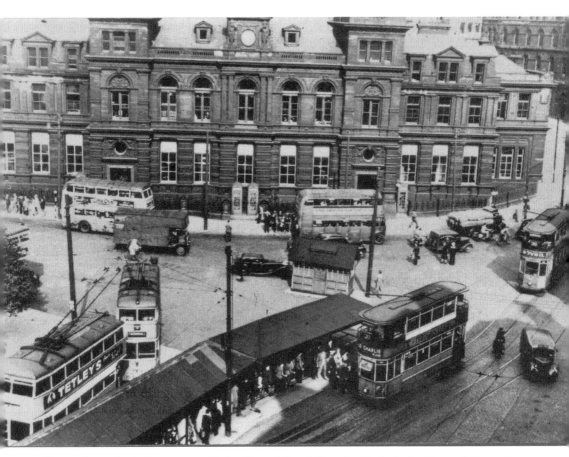

Forster Square in the late 1940s with the General Post Office of 1887 in the background. Trams for Bradford Moor plus a selection of trolleybuses and motor buses are also part of the scene. (*Author's collection*)

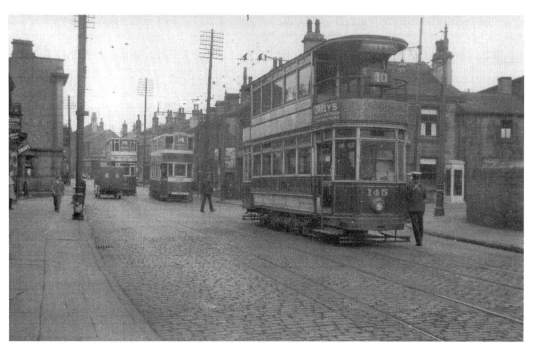

Bradford and Leeds trams meet at Stanningley. The two Leeds trams in the background are on the Leeds-to-Pudsey service. (*Author's collection*)

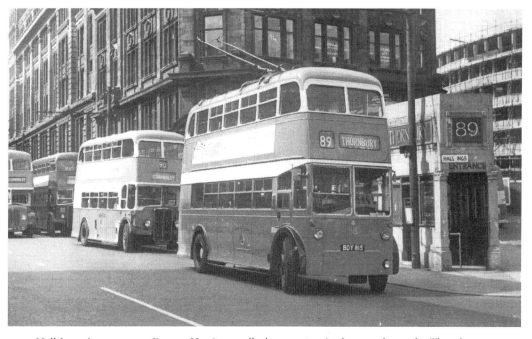

Hall Ings, August 1959. Former Hastings trolleybus no. 815 is about to depart for Thornbury. Two Stanningley buses stand behind while a Leeds City Transport AEC lurks in the background. To the right is the waiting shelter, which was christened 'Tut's Tomb' by the locals. (*Author's collection*)

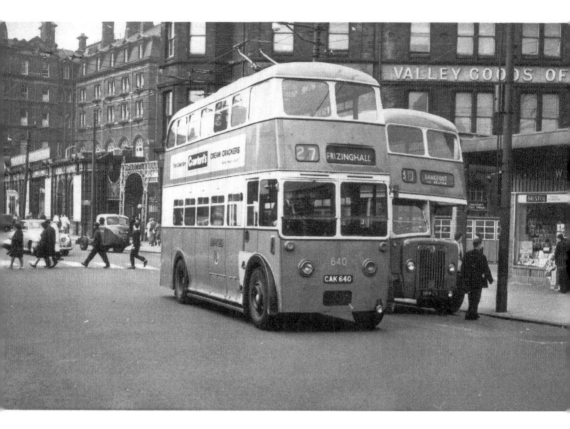

Forster Square, 16 October 1962. Trolleybus no. 640 is on its way around the square to commence a journey to Frizinghall. To the right, motor bus no. 79 is on the Bankfoot via Heaton route. Valley Road Goods Depot in the background would soon be demolished. (*Author's collection*)

CHAPTER TEN

Bradford Transport Preserved

When the last tram ran in Bradford on 6 May 1950, most people thought the tramway era was over, with the exception of a small group of enthusiasts with other ideas. Following the closure, tram no. 104 had taken up residence at Odsal Stadium, where it was in use as a scoreboard. In 1953 they decided to preserve the tram and it was returned to Thornbury Works where restoration began, and in July 1958 it was returned to use on the works approach track at Thornbury. It made a number of public appearances until 1963, and was eventually placed on display at the Industrial Museum at Moorside Mills, Eccleshill, in 1975.

One other Bradford tram remains in existence. This is no. 251 of 1920, which later ran in Sheffield between 1942 and 1951 as their no. 330. It was then cut down for use as a works car and served in this capacity until 1960, when it moved to the Tramway Museum at Crich in Derbyshire. It can still be seen there today, although it is restored to its Sheffield condition as no. 330 and does not carry passengers.

By the time the trolleybuses were coming to an end in the early 1970s, the preservation movement was well-established, and around twenty-five were purchased for preservation, though sadly a number of restoration projects have since fallen by the wayside. The Corporation put aside one vehicle, no. 737, for display at the Industrial Museum. Many others ended up at what is now the Trolleybus Museum at Sandtoft, which was established not far from Doncaster in 1969. Since that time, a number have been restored to running order and can be seen in operation at the museum's open days. Others remain as long-term restoration projects, such as English Electric-built single decker no. 562 of 1929.

Surprisingly, there are not a lot of Bradford motor buses in preservation. The earliest to survive is Leyland Lion no. 325 of 1927. The rare Leyland Lioness, no. 380 of 1929, was exported to the USA with a replica body some years ago and its present whereabouts are not known. Among post-war survivors are Leyland PD2 no. 558 of 1950, AEC Regent III no. 82 of 1952, former London Transport RT class no. 410 of 1947, plus a number of the many AEC Regent Vs of the 1960s. Examples of the later Leyland PD3s, Atlanteans and Daimler Fleetlines also made it into preservation.

The former Corporation bus depot at Ludlam Street, off Manchester Road, became the headquarters of the West Yorkshire Transport Museum between 1984 and 1993. This was intended as a temporary base prior to the construction of a major new venue at Low Moor, which eventually opened as Transperience in July 1995. A large collection of local vehicles was built up, but the new museum was a costly failure, lasting only a couple of years. The collection was eventually dispersed to other museums, including the Keighley Bus Museum, and to private individuals.

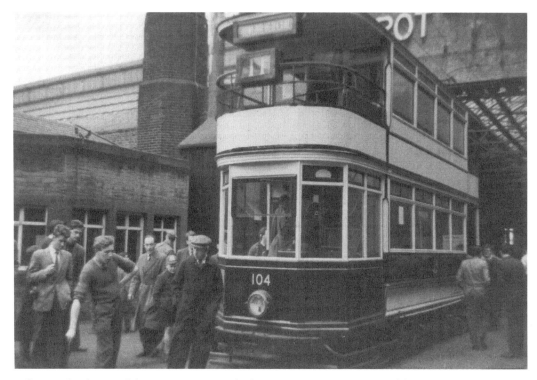

Following the closure of the tramway system, the last tram, no. 104, was rescued for preservation, and between 1958 and 1963 ran occasional trips at Thornbury Depot. It was put on display at the new Industrial Museum in 1975. (*Author's collection*)

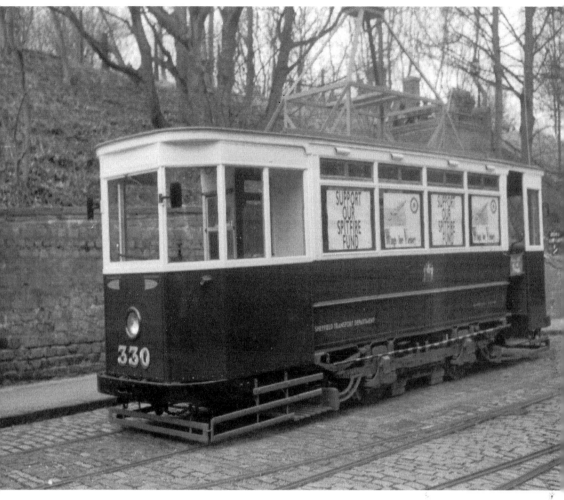

In 1942, ten Bradford trams were sold to Sheffield. They ran there until after the war, when no. 330 (formerly Bradford 251) was cut down for use as a works car. It survives to this day at the National Tramway Museum at Crich in Derbyshire. (*Author's collection*)

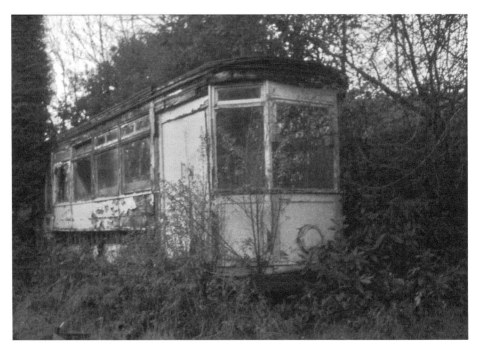

The lower deck of Bradford tramcar no. 54 survived in Thornton for many years. It is seen here in December 1984 before it was moved to secure storage for eventual restoration. (*Author's collection*)

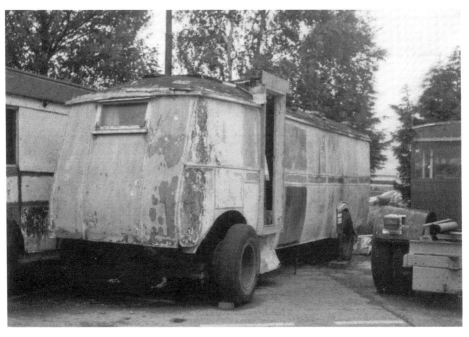

Yes, this was once a Bradford trolleybus – no. 562, an English Electric single decker of 1929, to be precise. On withdrawal in 1945, it served as a caravan for many years and is now awaiting restoration at the Trolleybus Museum at Sandtoft. (*Author's collection*)

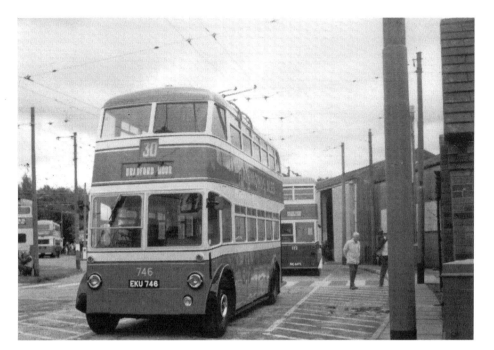

Among a number of Bradford trolleybuses in preservation is Roe-bodied BUT no. 746 of 1949. This vehicle now operates at the Trolleybus Museum and is here photographed in 2008. (*Author's collection*)

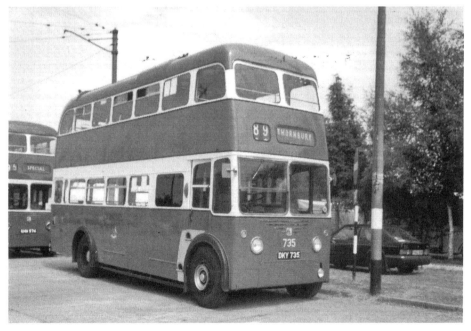

Taking a break between trips at the Trolleybus Museum is Bradford trolleybus no. 735. New in 1946, it was re-bodied with this East Lancashire Coachbuilders front-entrance body in 1959 and ran in service in Bradford until 1972. (*Author's collection*)

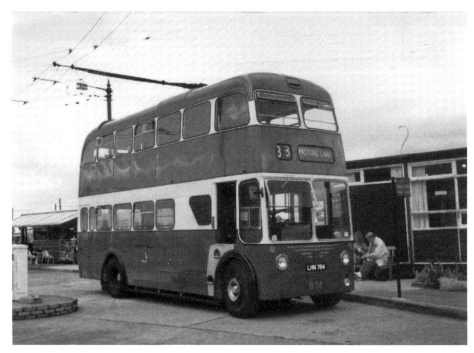

No. 834 was one of five 'third-hand' vehicles operated by Bradford. New in 1949 to Darlington, they moved on to Doncaster in 1952 and reached Bradford in 1962. Given attractive East Lancashire bodies before entering service, they only ran for ten years in Bradford. It is seen awaiting passengers at the Trolleybus Museum. (*Author's collection*)

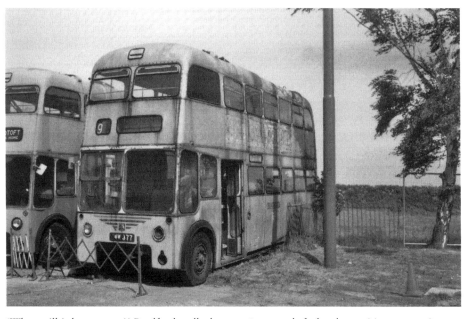

'When will it be my turn?' Bradford trolleybus no. 847 stands forlornly awaiting restoration at the Trolleybus Museum in 2008. (*Author's collection*)

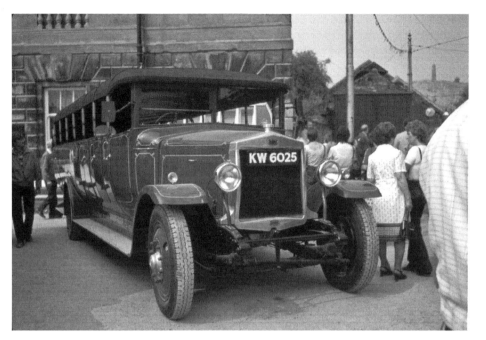

This is the Leyland Lioness bus KW 6025, which we saw in Chapter Six after being fitted with a replica charabanc body. It is seen here at the National Tramway Museum at Crich before being exported to the United States. (*Author's collection*)

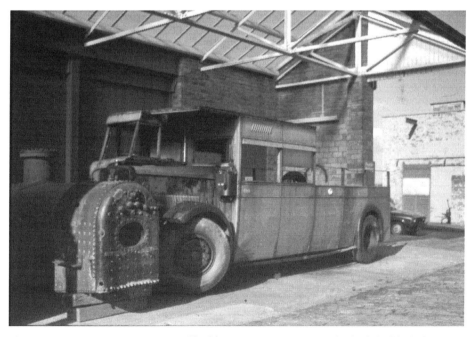

This 1935 AEC Regent was once Bradford bus no. 401, a Weymann-bodied double decker. In 1954, it was converted into a grit lorry and after many years at Bradford Industrial Museum it is now housed at the Keighley Bus Museum. (*Author's collection*)

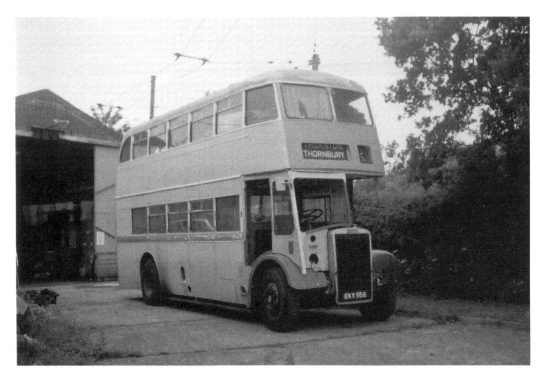

Leyland-bodied Leyland Titan PD2 no. 558 of 1949 is undergoing restoration at the Trolleybus Museum, as seen in this 2009 view, and will soon be as good as new. (*Author's collection*)

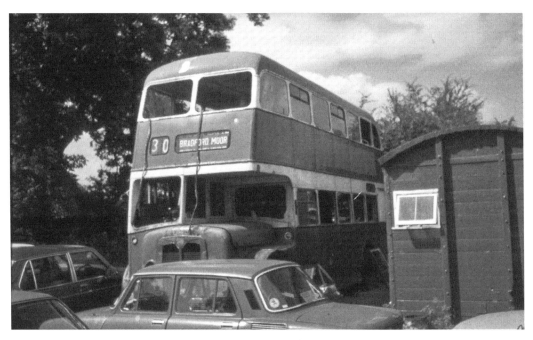

One of forty AEC Regent IIIs with East Lancashire bodywork new to Bradford in 1952-53, no. 82 awaits restoration at Sandtoft in the 1980s. (*Author's collection*)

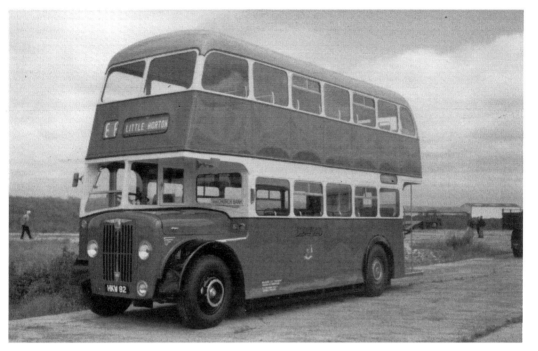

Now restored to its original condition, complete with grey roof, no. 82 is seen attending a rally at the Trolleybus Museum. (*Author's collection*)

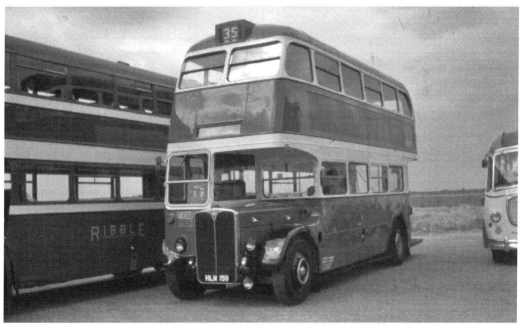

On withdrawal in 1963, no. 410, one of the former London Transport RTs, passed into preservation. It is still an active participant on the rally scene in 2010. It is seen here attending the Sandtoft Gathering back in 1986. (*Author's collection*)

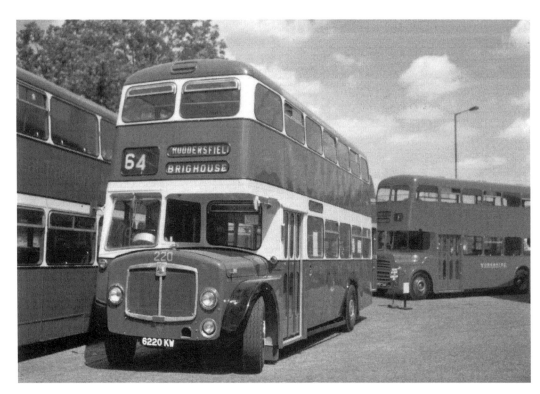

Typical of the 120 AEC Regent V motor buses that dominated the Corporation bus fleet in the 1960s and 1970s is no. 220, which is now preserved. The red bus behind belonged to the Yorkshire Woollen District Transport Company. (*Author's collection*)

CHAPTER ELEVEN
A Transport Miscellany

And so we come to the 'odds and ends' section, which includes things that don't really belong anywhere else.

Over the years, a number of buses and trams have found shelter in Bradford, using the city as a stopping-off point to somewhere else.

We have already mentioned the ill-fated Transperience museum project, where a number of Bradford's own vehicles were on display. Due to the low bridge in Cleckheaton Road, double-deck vehicles could not be used on the museum's internal service, and so an interesting assortment of foreign vehicles were used.

From time to time, historic vehicle rallies are staged in or pass through the city, such as the annual Trans-Pennine Run. These feature a wide variety of beautifully restored vehicles, including some from the local area.

Bus and tram systems need a fleet of maintenance vehicles for when things go wrong, and these often have interesting histories.

Special vehicles not used for ordinary bus services are often used to transport disabled children to and from school.

An interesting experiment in October and November 2005 saw the 'Bradford Minitram Shuttle', which involved the use of a small battery-powered bus on a service around the centre of the city. It seemed to struggle up the hills just like the people of Bradford do!

Finally there is the question of what happens to old, worn-out buses and trams. Only the fortunate few go on to be preserved; the rest go for scrap. Some, however, take longer to get there, having a variety of uses along the way.

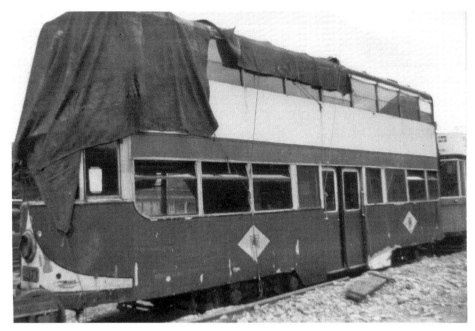

This Sunderland tram, no. 100, spent some years in storage at Thornbury Works before finding a permanent home at the Tramway Museum at Crich in Derbyshire, where it is seen here. It was originally new to the Metropolitan Electric Tramways in London in 1930 and is now restored as MET car no. 331. (*Author's collection*)

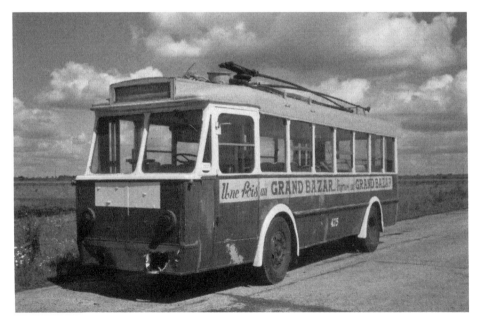

This former Liège trolleybus, no. 425, was built in 1932. For some years it was kept in the Bradford area and was once seen running under the wires in Wakefield Road. Following restoration, it is the oldest working vehicle at the Trolleybus Museum, where it is seen here. (*Author's collection*)

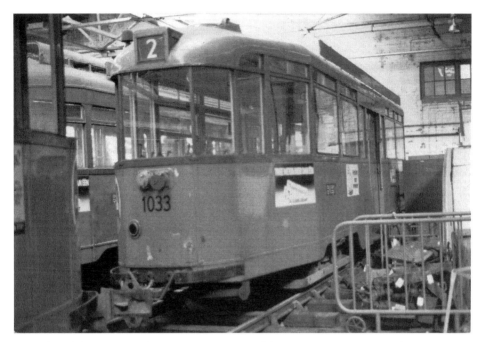

A number of former Rotterdam trams were acquired for operation on a proposed tramway in the Spen Valley, near Bradford. They were stored at the West Yorkshire Transport Museum in the former Ludlam Street bus depot. This is trailer car no. 1033, which was new in 1949. Their present whereabouts are unknown. (*Author's collection*)

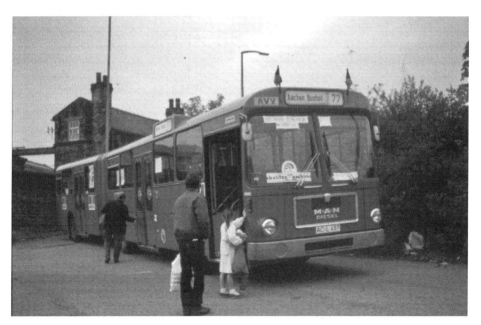

This MAN articulated single decker from Aachen, Germany, was a frequent visitor to the West Yorkshire Transport Museum in the 1980s. Similar articulated buses later operated in Bradford on the Allerton to Holme Wood route. (*Author's collection*)

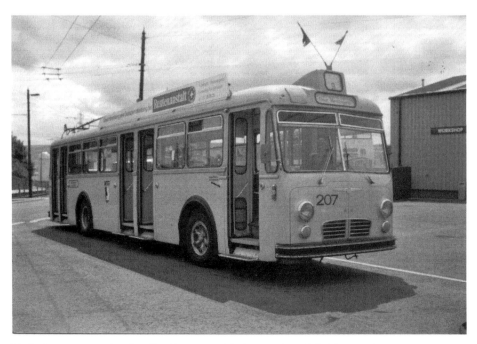

Trolleybuses returned to Bradford in 1995 with the opening of the Transperience museum at Low Moor. This former Schaffhausen trolleybus was new to Lucerne. Sadly the museum was not a success and had closed by 1998. (*Author's collection*)

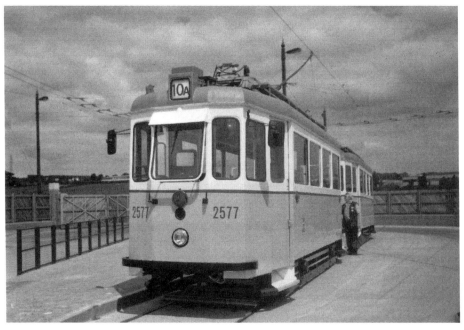

A low bridge at Transperience meant that only single-deck vehicles could be operated. This former Budapest tram and trailer dating from 1904 are seen operating the short service along the museum site. (*Author's collection*)

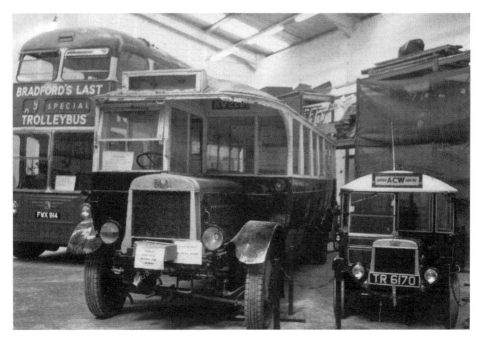

Also displayed at Transperience was Bradford's last trolleybus, no. 844, plus this 1927 Leyland Lion motor bus, which ran in Bradford until 1936. To the right is a scale model of the Leyland Lion that was used for publicity purposes by a local garden centre. (*Author's collection*)

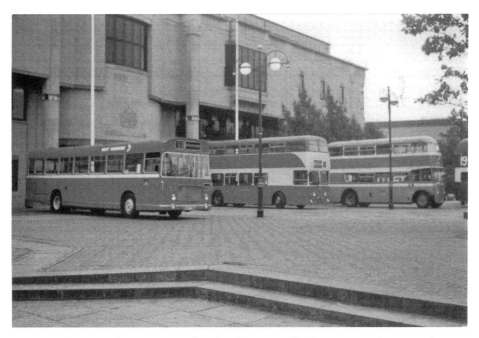

Displays of historic vehicles occasionally take place in Bradford city centre. This September 2002 line-up outside the new Law Courts includes buses from the former West Yorkshire, Huddersfield and Halifax fleets. (*Author's collection*)

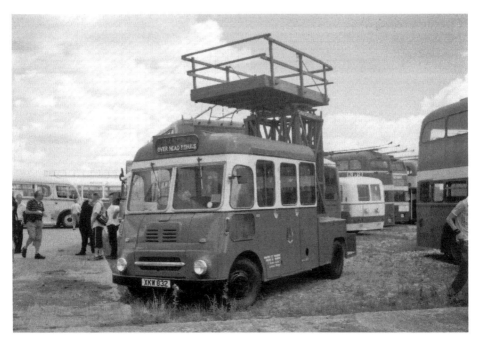

Special vehicles were needed to maintain Bradford's tram and trolleybus overhead wiring. This Austin FGK60 tower wagon was new in 1962 but when the trolleys ended in 1972 it found a new home at the Trolleybus Museum at Sandtoft. Health and safety legislation has rendered it redundant again, and it has been replaced by a 'cherry picker'. (*Author's collection*)

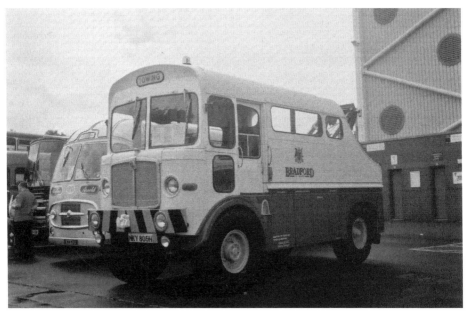

Broken-down buses needed specialised breakdown trucks to move them. This is Bradford's AEC Matador, NKY 805H. New in 1947, it was fitted with this modern-looking bodywork in the 1970s, and is now preserved. (*Author's collection*)

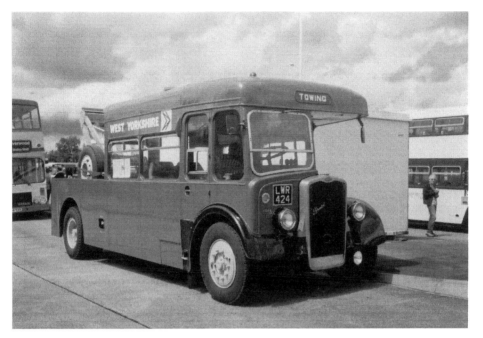

West Yorkshire converted this former double-deck bus into their Bradford towing vehicle in 1972. It was originally bus no. DGW 4, a Bristol KSW6G dating from 1953. (*Author's collection*)

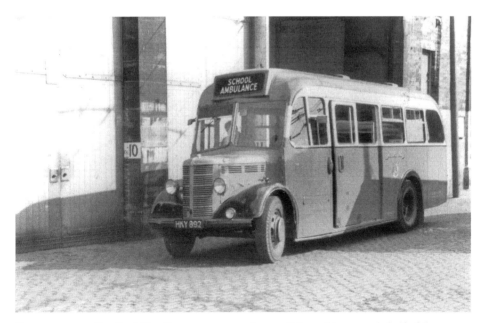

For many years, Bradford City Transport operated a small fleet of buses on behalf of the Education Department. They were used to take disabled children to special schools. Here, rare Bedford OLAZ HKY 892 with Roe bodywork is seen outside Thornbury Depot. It was used from 1953 to 1971. (*Author's collection*)

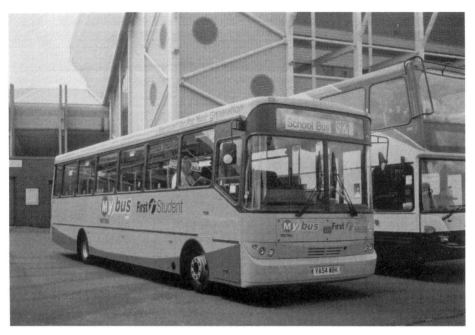

Present-day transport for many local children is the specially designed school buses built by BMC in Turkey. Each pupil has a designated seat with a seat belt, and each bus has a regular driver. (*Author's collection*)

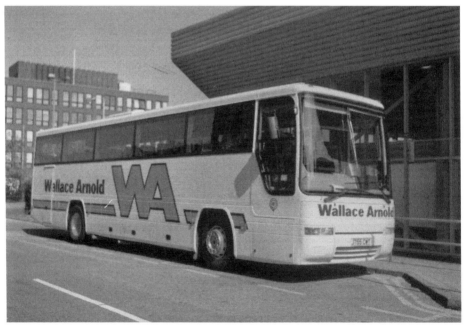

Wallace Arnold coaches were a familiar sight in Bradford on their holiday tours. This Plaxton-bodied Volvo, J755 CWT, is seen in Leicester during a journey back to West Yorkshire. Wallace Arnold merged with Shearings in 1995. (*Author's collection*)

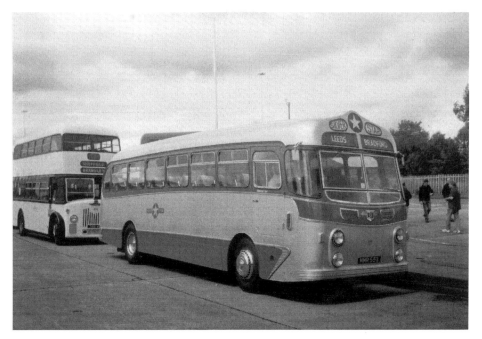

During the 1950s and early 1960s, many forces' leave services were operated around Britain. This stylish Harrington-bodied Leyland Tiger Cub owned by Silver Star Motor Services of Porton Down, near Salisbury, was a regular performer on services to Leeds and Bradford. It is now restored to its original condition and is seen here in 2009. (*Author's collection*)

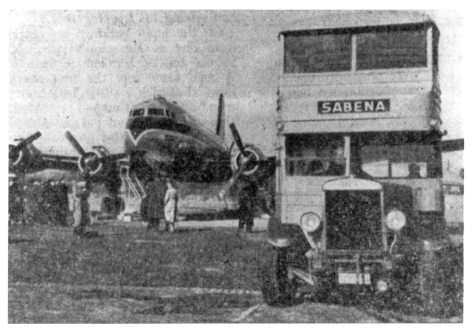

Old buses never die (1). This former Bradford Corporation Leyland TD1 of 1928 was one of two sold to the Belgian national airline SABENA in 1945. (*Author's collection*)

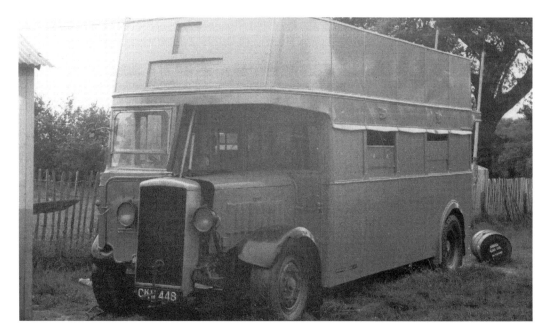

Old buses never die (2). This English Electric-bodied Daimler COG6, CKW 448, was new to Bradford in 1939. Following withdrawal in 1952, it was used by several showmen around the north of England before being scrapped in 1962. Note how the top deck and rear platform have been removed. (*Author's collection*)

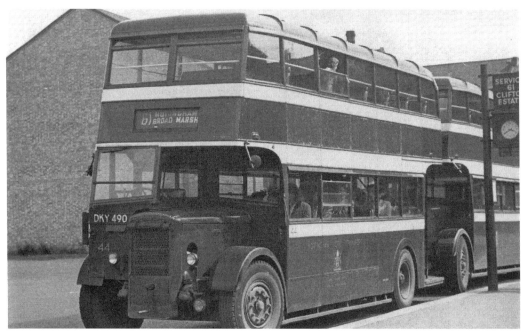

Old buses never die (3). Nottingham Corporation purchased seven former Bradford buses in 1952. This was formerly Bradford no. 490, a Daimler CWA6 with low-height Duple bodywork new in 1945. It ran in Nottingham until 1958. (*R. F. Mack*)

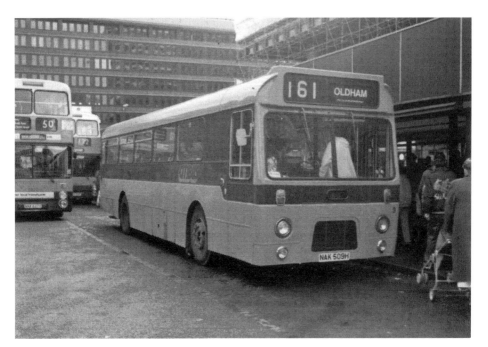

Old buses never die (4). This Marshall-bodied Leyland Panther was new to Bradford City Transport in 1969 as no. 509. It was later sold to Citibus of Oldham, with whom it is seen in Piccadilly Gardens, Manchester. (*Author's collection*)

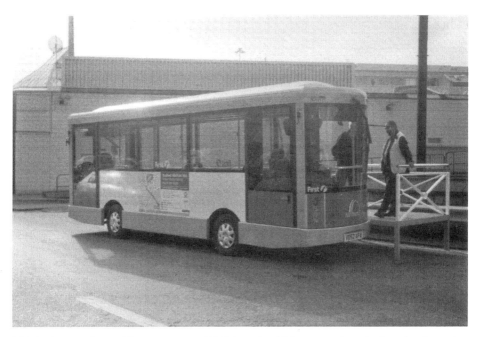

This is the experimental battery-powered 'Minitram', which was used on the free shuttle service in Bradford in 2005. Although it seemed like a good idea at the time, walking was still quicker! (*Author's collection*)

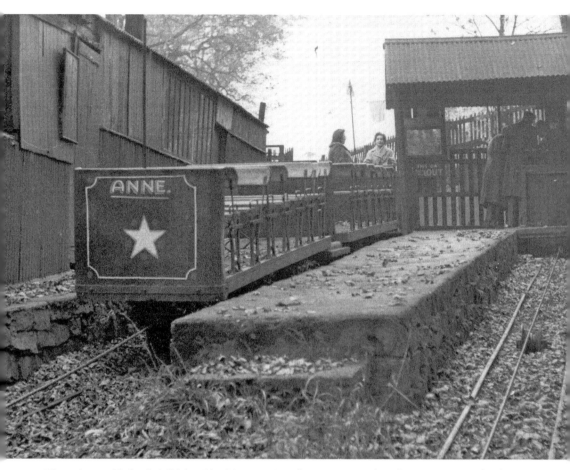

The unique cable-hauled Shipley Glen Tramway is still in operation, though it now attracts far fewer visitors than it did in its heyday when a day out on the Glen was a popular pastime. For some years, the two cars were named 'Anne' and 'Charles', after the royal children. (*R. F. Mack*)

Further Reading

The principal histories of the Bradford transport system are the three volumes by well-known local transport historian Stanley King:

Bradford Corporation Trolleybuses (Venture Publications, 1994).
Bradford Corporation Motor Buses (Venture Publications, 1995).
Bradford Corporation Tramways (Venture Publications, 1998).

Also by Stanley King is *Transport of Delight: The Bradford Trolleybus System, 1911-72* (National Trolleybus Association, 1972).

Other books on the city's trams are:

Bradford Tramways by D. J. Croft (Oakwood Press, 1976).
Bradford City Tramways, 1882-1950 by D. M. Coates (Wyvern Publications, 1984).

The trolleybuses have received a lot of coverage, and the following books can be recommended:

The Bradford Trolleybus System by J. A. L. Stainforth and H. Brearley (West Riding Transport Society, 1972). This 188-page book contains chapters on routes, a detailed fleet history, and, most useful of all, plenty of maps and overhead wiring diagrams.

Bradford Trolleybuses by Stephen Lockwood (Middleton Press, 2003).
Bradford and Its Trolleybuses by Geoff Lumb (Venture Publications, 2006).

There is also an interesting series of books by Stan Ledgard. *Early Turn, Split Turn* and *Late Turn* (Bobtail Press, 2006) deal with Bradford trolleybuses between 1960 and 1972, and *Show Up* and *Nannying* (Bobtail Press, 2007) deal with Bradford trolleybuses and motor buses between 1960 and 1975.

For those interested in the vehicles themselves, the PSV Circle's *Fleet History of Bradford Corporation*, published in 1993, contains full details of all the trams, trolleybuses, motor buses and ancillary vehicles.

ALSO AVAILABLE FROM
AMBERLEY PUBLISHING

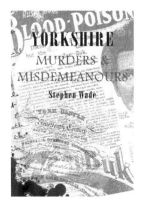

YORKSHIRE MURDERS & MISDEMEANOURS

Stephen Wade

Price: £12.99
ISBN: 978-1-84868-559-8
Binding: PB
Extent: 128 pages

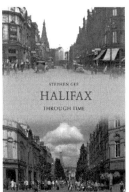

HALIFAX THROUGH TIME

Stephen Gee

Price: £14.99
ISBN: 978-1-4456-0241-7
Binding: PB
Extent: 96 pages
Full colour throughout

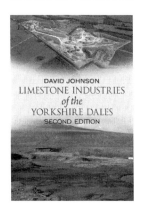

LIMESTONE INDUSTRIES OF THE YORKSHIRE DALES

David Johnson

Price: £18.99
ISBN: 978-1-4456-0060-4
Binding: PB
Extent: TBC

AVAILABLE FROM ALL GOOD BOOKSHOPS OR ORDER DIRECT
FROM OUR WEBSITE WWW.AMBERLEYBOOKS.COM